"It is a joy to see that Jane Rutter is offering the results of her prayerful reflections to help us all as we progress through the liturgical year. I am certain that all who avail themselves of *Seasons of the Spirit* will be greatly rewarded with God's grace and peace."

Most Reverend John R. Gaydos
Bishop of Jefferson City

"Jane Rutter in her book *Seasons of the Spirit* has beautifully captured how our souls are regenerated through the dailiness of our lives to resemble the spirit of Jesus Christ and identify with God's purpose. This book is a profound and transforming piece of literature! This book is life changing. A must read!"

"Women in God's Service" Bible Study Group

"*Seasons of the Spirit* touched me deeply. Jane opens doors that others may enter and in so doing, experience a sharing of the heart that is precious."

Barb Dowding
Associate Chancellor
Archdiocese of Vancouver

G000066270

Seasons of the Spirit

Reflections on Finding God in Daily Life

E. Jane Rutter

LITURGICAL PRESS

Collegeville, Minnesota

www.litpress.org

ISBN 978-0-8146-4918-3   ISBN 978-0-8146-3853-8 (ebook)

We are blessed to live where one season leads to the next, assured that spring will turn to summer, summer to fall, fall to winter, and winter to spring. Tree branches awaken and flower, shed their leaves, and lay dormant until they bloom again. Our church parallels nature; its seasons never falter.

June 2021

Contents

Advent

Lent

Easter

Ordinary Time

ADVENT

1 *All Is New*

This weekend, we open the door to a new month, a new year, and a renewed commitment to our faith. As we turn our calendars to the month of December, we also enter into the church's new liturgical year, marked by the first week of Advent.

And what a wonderful reading we begin with at Mass, the prophet Isaiah telling us of his vision of the future of Judah and Jerusalem! His words inspire us to look up, to set our eyes and our efforts on that which is above.

"In days to come / the mountain of the LORD's house / shall be established as the highest of the mountains, / and shall be raised above the hills" (Isa 2:2). His words speak to people of every age, reminding us that our purpose is to reach the peak, the Lord's house, where our hearts reside. Isaiah's imagery is of God looking down on us from the mountain, our instructor, judge, and arbitrator, perhaps invoking in us a God that is distant and removed from our lives.

But, no, we needn't limit ourselves so. Isaiah invites us to "go up to the mountain of the LORD, / to the house of the God of Jacob; / that he may teach us his ways / and that we may walk in his paths" (Isa 2:3). We are invited to walk together to God's house—peoples of all nations. It is in God's house that we will find our commonality through love. We will desist from fighting to accept God's way of peace.

Each step we climb up the mountain we put sin behind us and grow ever stronger in the purity of love that is God. We recommit to our faith with wiser eyes and loving hearts.

Simply stated, Isaiah's prophecy is a fantastic purpose statement for our walk on this earth that we can renew every year! Next year, I will

1. lift my eyes in prayer to God;
2. go to the house of the Lord;
3. embrace learning;
4. invite others to walk with me;
5. open my heart to peace;
6. grow in love.

And so I pray: Dear Lord, help me walk up the mountain to your house, that I may always live in you.

2 *Conference Planning*

I spent two days in Chicago this week serving on the conference planning committee for the International Catholic Stewardship Council. Gathered together with forty colleagues—stewardship directors and priests from the United States and Canada—volunteering their gifts to set the program sessions that people worldwide will flock to for instruction and inspiration on living in Christ.

In the unlikely setting of a meeting room this first week of Advent, I find myself walking up the mountain to God's home with people of all nations (Isa 2:2-3). To be a part of this group is humbling, energizing, and spiritually uplifting. For they are people who love God, coming together with a single focus: to proclaim Christ to others.

At Mass this second week of Advent, we will hear the words of justice and peace, and harmony and praise. We will be challenged to produce good fruit. I will think of the young man sitting beside me on the El train, immersed in his Bible. Wanting to make that Christian connection, I asked him what verse he was reading in Proverbs. He looked up and responded to me with a gentleness in his eyes and voice that didn't correspond to his stained teeth or haggard-looking face. Again, I met Christ in the unlikely setting of the El as it clattered above the hotels, neighborhoods, and industrial sections of the city.

And so I pray: Dear Lord, let this Advent be one of open eyes and hearts, that I may see your face in unlikely settings and proclaim your love in truth.

3   *Club Stewardship vs. Church Stewardship*

There are times when I entertain the thought that our parishes and diocese should start a "club stewardship." We could host weekly games and shows so members would give us their time, use volunteer help so members would give us their talent, and operate the club on dues so our financial needs would always be met. Club stewardship would be a self-supporting, fun, and personally profitable place to go!

While operating a club has these stated benefits, church stewardship's foundation and premise are inherently different than that of club stewardship:

- Club stewardship is a social gathering where one goes to have fun, but also to be seen by others of equal or greater status. Church stewardship invites everyone in on equal footing as children of God, regardless of status, membership, financial portfolio, race, age, gender, or even attitude.

- Club stewardship relies on volunteers who often give their time in return for meeting contacts with whom they can do business in other settings. Church stewardship is filled with stewards who give their time to serve others as Christ did, not for personal gain.

- Club stewardship selects its members by their financial ability. Church stewardship serves the poor and wealthy alike.

Clubs have their place of value in our lives. We do have fun watching sports competitions, playing games, meeting business associates, and generally enjoying ourselves. However, we cannot mistake the temporal pleasures or business gains we experience at clubs as substitutes for the true sense of stewardship that only a relationship with God offers. It is through church stewardship that we gain a deep sense of God's love, peace, and community that is everlasting.

Most important, church stewardship is founded on the Gospel values of recognizing that everything we have comes from God, and, in our gratefulness, we return the firstfruits of our labor to God—through our time, talent, and treasure.

Church stewardship requires a conversion of heart. A Christian steward is defined by the United States Conference of Catholic Bishops as "one who receives God's gifts gratefully, cherishes and tends them in a responsible and accountable manner, shares them in justice and love with others, and returns them with increase to the Lord" (Stewardship: A Disciple's Response, V).

Advent is a time of waiting for Christ and can be a fitting time to examine our personal stewardship by reflecting on the following seven questions:

1. Is our primary time spent in jobs or social arenas where we are uncomfortable practicing or expressing our faith?

2. Do we spend time with our children, family, and friends in ways that honor God?

3. Do we serve others less fortunate than ourselves?

4. Do we teach our children, and are we learning about the rich catechism, history, and traditions of Catholicism?

5. Do we use our talents to their fullest capacity?

6. Are we allocating our financial resources to support the needs of our church in thanksgiving to God's gifts to us?

7. Are we inviting and guiding others to the eucharistic table?

To actively engage in this reflection process, consider scheduling individual time or holding a family meeting within the next few weeks to explore these seven questions. Develop a personal plan of action for yourself and/or your family, defining steps you can take to enrich your stewardship. You may choose a simple format such as the following:

- read an individual question;
- ask each individual to write down his/her thoughts regarding that question;
- share your thoughts openly with each other;
- develop an action plan by asking, "What can we do to respond to God?" and writing down specific actions you will take.

A conversion of our hearts to stewardship enhances our realization and acceptance of God's presence and guidance in every aspect of our lives. Simply stated, as joyful stewards, we act out of gratitude for God's love.

4   *Unfailing Support*

Halloween is past, Thanksgiving is past, and Christmas is already here. On my way home from work every evening, I pass by plastic Santas and red-colored lights twinkling at me from front yards. I weed out the ad inserts from the newspaper, throwing them into the trash can before I bring the paper into the house to read. Number one—Christmas isn't remotely here yet. Number two—what I don't see, I won't be tempted to buy. Number three—I keep trying to switch my focus from "It's Beginning to Look a Lot Like Christmas" to "O Little Town of Bethlehem."

The gift I love to receive is time with my family. It is a goal I seek throughout the seasons, and one my mother and siblings recognize as important to me. Call it the desire to give "unfailing support of one another." We offer that petition at Mass, recognizing we are a family, a community of faith, built on the cross of Christ and the foundation of Peter.

Jesus, however, claimed to come with a sword that would split families apart. As we approach the holiday season, we witness families lost in past bitterness and blame. Somewhere on the path, they shut down their spiritual connections and quit reaching out to one another. They lost their ability to see the good and to nurture Christ in one another.

Without Jesus, Thanksgiving and Christmas become the season of "unmet expectations." Nothing we receive is quite what we wanted, the people we party with seem stale, we wrangle with irritating crowds in the stores to get the first crack at this year's new and glittery whatever. Nothing completely satisfies the emptiness within.

5 *Comfort*

"Comfort, give comfort to my people, / says your God," Isaiah shares with us (Isa 40:1, NABRE).

What a great message for us to embrace. We need comfort from fear of the financial recession and its impact on us, comfort from dire news messages that we subliminally inhale, comfort in this time of change within our political landscape.

As a nation we are consumed in a knee-jerk reaction of fearing what we cannot control, anticipating the worst, and publicly scattering seeds of blame that grow like thorns. The same reactions have held true in every nation long before Christ's coming as man.

Isaiah counters this age-old doom with God's words of comfort.

We may think it naive or Pollyannaish to walk lightly and spread any good news (much less the Good News) in the midst of uncertainty. But, as Christians, we are called, even chosen, for this mission. Isaiah ends this beautiful psalm with the following balm:

They that hope in the LORD will renew their strength,
    they will soar on eagles' wings;
They will run and not grow weary,
    walk and not grow faint. (40:31, NABRE)

As believers in and followers of Christ, we are gifted with spirits of faith to go out and give comfort. All need the comfort of the Word, some the comfort of food and shelter, others the comfort of work and family.

This spirit of selflessness reigns in and among all our communities. Flowing from the Eucharist, it is evidenced in our relationships with one another, the sacrificial sharing of our material goods, the desire to give rather than receive, knowing the latter is the greater gift.

Herein we experience the joy that bubbles out from deep within us, regardless of the world's current state of affairs. Suffering comes and goes in our life. Joy is always within us, coming to the surface whenever we forget ourselves and, as Christ, reach out to others.

Don't let us forget we belong to God. This holy season let's celebrate the coming of the Lord Jesus Christ. Meet our brother, sister, mother, and Father at Mass. Cloak us in the Eucharist. Place our church's needs at the forefront of giving from what we have.

And so I pray: Dear God, stay with us, ever present within our hearts and leading our actions. Help us find our joy in abandoning our comfort for others.

6 *Gratitude*

To be overcome by gratitude is a marvelous feeling. Taking personal inventory of our year, I bet the good things outweigh the bad; the glass is half full; God gave us the strength to handle our circumstances, and the grace to look for the silver lining.

That grace is so important. For if at first our inventory list seems filled with rain, when we sincerely open ourselves to God, asking to understand the lessons our experiences hold for us, and how we are to use these insights in his service, we can only be humbled and strengthened. Gratitude doesn't mean the sun will shine for us every day.

There are times we may feel isolated from love and community and think we have been shortchanged. We forget how to love; we feel lost and in need of step-by-step instructions to finally learn to love the right way. God the parent smiles in affection, unveiling the answer in simplicity. "I gave you my son, Jesus." Oh yes, we blush in humble remembrance: look to Jesus.

Expressing our gratitude for the gift of his Son is what this season of Advent is about. It is a time to opt for loving to serve and serving to love, to admit our failings and so be freed from them, to put aside petty jealousies and positioning, to release our anxieties.

Prior to our final response to the Our Father at Mass, we hear the priest pray, "Deliver us, Lord, we pray, from every evil, / graciously grant peace in our days, / that, by the help of your mercy, / we may be always free from sin / and safe from all distress, / as we await the blessed hope / and the coming of our Savior, Jesus Christ."

To accept peace and protection from anxiety, we must also accept that by opening the door to a relationship with our Creator, we are never alone. Psalm 139 affirms this. "For it was you who formed my inward parts; / you knit me together in my mother's womb. / I praise you, for I am fearfully and wonderfully made" (vv. 13-14). This Advent finally accept that you are a beloved son or daughter of God.

Saint Teresa of Avila confirms the experiences of the psalmist, telling us in *The Way of Perfection*, "He refuses to force our will. He takes what we give Him but does not give Himself wholly until He sees that we are giving ourselves entirely to Him."[1] We only truly serve in God's name when we are strong enough in faith to believe in ourselves wholly as gifts of God, and have an overwhelming desire to give the gift of God to others. Service is a glorious gift God has graced us with.

And so I pray: Lord, we have much for which to be grateful. This Advent let us be invigorated by your love, dear Lord. Renew our service in your fold.

Note

1. Saint Teresa of Avila, *The Way of Perfection*, ed. Henry L. Carrigan Jr. (Brewster, MA: Paraclete Press, 2000), 124–25.

7 *Painting*

Perhaps because they happen infrequently, I savor snow days. The fifteen-inch pileup that surrounded us the first week of Advent gave me the rare gift of four days to sleep in, pad around in my slippers, bake bread, hang out with David and Laura, and . . . *paint.*

Family coming for Christmas served as our incentive to delve into repainting most rooms, installing a tile shower, and wallpapering.

As with everything, the task of painting involves ritual. There is the donning of comfortable sweats that would pass for rags elsewhere than home, making fresh coffee to keep a good supply of caffeine pumping through the veins, and playing *White Christmas* with the volume on the television set blasting so the sounds of Rosemary Clooney and Bing Crosby reverberate through the house.

With the mood set, the rhythm of painting takes over. It is an elegant symmetry between the repetitive movement of brush in hand and the mind emptying to invite God in. Time and schedules are replaced with the color and thoughts that I paint on my canvas wall.

I think of my husband, children, and the rest of our family. My children are always at the forefront of my prayers. As a mother, I look to Mary, asking her to hold them in her arms and lead them to her son, Jesus the Christ. Long ago, I realized the only prayer that matters to mothers is for their children to accept God. There is an incredible peace in knowing that whatever else happens in their lives—the joys and sorrows—bears little import against our children's acceptance to discipleship.

We begin this Advent season called to be on guard for the coming of Christ, assured that he will fill us with joy and laughter. Sitting on the floor painting the trim, I am overcome with the sensation of being blessed. Sharing Christmas with my family gathered in body and spirit is a gift that, like snow days, happens too infrequently. Our love is like Christ's, given freely and with open heart. Though we share the similarity of blood and background, our paths vary widely. Not all have accepted Christ, and that longing and hope stay with me.

Picking up a wet cloth, I wipe paint speckles off my hands and look around the room. I hear Rosemary and Bing sing, "May your days be merry and bright," while opening the doors of inn's stage to reveal snow falling. In the fields of Vermont and my home, everything looks fresh, clean, and inviting.

And so I pray: May our home serve as praise to you, dear Lord, its comfort and warmth inviting all to come to you. Fill this home with your love and spirit.

8   *Skipping Christmas*

I am years behind on reading John Grisham's *Skipping Christmas*, but I was captured by its title in the book section of Gerbes while frantically grocery shopping Sunday night among a passel of college students. There is a wonderful allure to the thought of skipping Christmas with its hyper-frenzied overindulging state of shopping, cooking, spending, cleaning, eating, and partying. Already tired from the fullness of fall's schedule, it is rest from all that fills my dreams.

Having just begun the book, I won't speculate on how the story ends, but instead give some thought on how to keep the season in line with the goal to follow Christ more nearly:

> Realize how much we have: The refrigerator is stocked, the house is warm, and we are well clothed. Not only are we comfortable, but richer than peoples of many other nations. We are blessed with a loving family and friends, jobs, and a life of freedom.

> Embrace the concept of less is better: Down to one credit card, we pay the charges off monthly. We've forewarned

our local banker to look toward the next generation for business as our only goal is to pay off our mortgage. We are saving cash for a new-to-us car, hoping the Toyota will last another year beyond its current 200,000 miles.

Keep less and give more: We don't miss what we give and certainly are not sacrificing. We've chosen to tithe to our parish and diocese automatically through our checking account. Giving up possessing a new car or toys or vacations cannot be called sacrifice, so we make an effort not to relate one to the other. We desire plenty, but need little.

Focus on Advent at home and church: We light the wreath at the dinner table, pray as a family, put up the manger, and attend reconciliation services and Mass. We're teaching our children the traditions of our faith through its practice.

As Advent approaches, I think of the ways I have failed this year. Face-to-face with my own unworthiness, I need to ask for and receive forgiveness—to be cleansed in the birth of Christ. It is so humbling to be loved without reservation.

We will put up a tree and buy presents and bake cookies. We will celebrate. However, as the years go by and we try to follow Christ more nearly, the celebration gains in depth and in the realization of what an awesome gift God has given us in Christ and each other.

Please let me know how you are "skipping Christmas," but don't tell me how the book ends.

9 *Mary's Walk*

It is the Sabbath and we have paused on our journey to Bethlehem. Sheltered by the mountains, as evening sets we sit by the campfire letting its warmth seep through our tired bones. The baby in my womb is gentle as if sensing the time to rest is come. We will reach our destination soon enough. Thus settled, I return to the thoughts that bind me ever closer to the prophets of the Lord who foretold of this time.

I think of David the shepherd king marveling, "Who am I, O Lord GOD, and what is my house, that you have brought me thus far?" (2 Sam 7:18). From the depths of age, his words are planted in my heart and on my lips! For now I walk the path that God bequeathed to David, a servant in his house called to fulfill the Master's plan.

I bow low to the ground beneath me, breathing in the sweet earth God has created. I look up to the cedars, humbled by their might. Beyond, the stars and moon lift the darkness of night in glory to the greatness of the Lord. This is the house of David, the ancestor of Joseph. God claimed him long before he walked these hills and slept under this sky.

Just as he claimed me: "The young woman is with child and shall bear a son, and shall name him Immanuel" (Isa 7:14). When the angel came to me, how could I respond other than to say yes? For he has filled me with grace, the gift to bear the son on whose shoulders authority rests. The "Wonderful Counselor, Mighty God, / Everlasting Father, Prince of Peace" (Isa 9:6).

I wrap my cloak around me, chilled as I ponder the prophet's words: "His authority shall grow continually, / and there shall be endless peace / for the throne of David and his kingdom. / He will establish and uphold it / with justice and with righteousness / from this time onward and forevermore" (Isa 9:7).

Indeed, Joseph and I speak with great joy of the task that lies ahead of us, tending to this child who will grow to claim his predestined throne. How we shall present him at the temple, and raise him according to the traditional laws of Moses. And he shall bring peace and justice and righteousness to our people. How long we have waited, O Lord, for your reign to come!

You have brought us from the familiarity of our homes to a journey we scarcely understand to serve you in a manner we are most unworthy of. We are awed and filled with a grace we can hardly contain. Surely it shines out of our pores to light up the path.

Tomorrow we shall rise and continue our walk to Bethlehem. We end tonight in prayer: Give joy to your servant, O Lord, for to you I lift up my soul (Ps 89:1-37).

10 *Best Friends*

This morning I was thinking about best friends, considering all those whom I love. I have my husband, mother, siblings, children, and friends, but with whom do I share my deepest self? Of course, any Christian knows the Sunday school answer: Jesus/God is my best friend. Thinking this train of thought through, I realize that the exclusive best friend relationship we have with God is not meant to supplant our human relations, but serves as the model, the basis, for our friendships with others.

We rely on our friends much like we rely on God. We expect them to agree with us no matter what, to take our side, to always be here when we need them. But, there's a big difference between our relationship with God and our human friends. God will never let us down.

Whether right or wrong, God is always *by* our side, but not necessarily *on* our side. He will, in no uncertain terms, let us know when we are wrong and give us the action to correct that wrong. Which is to say, God is more than friend—he is parent. Today, it seems more parents opt for friendship with their kids rather than taking on the role of parenting. Parenting does not always make us act or feel warm and fuzzy.

David and I just took our kids to see Bill Cosby and we all laughed at the stories he told about his childhood. Clearly, his parents were the authority in his home. They were the guides and disciplinarians, set the rules, all with the goal of raising their children to become adults—by the time they could vote, no less!

"Eighteen and you're set to fly, kid" seems to have been the expectation in past generations. That's not to imply that parents of yesteryear didn't love or didn't have great relationships with their children; rather, it's more to say that the line between parent and friend wasn't blurred the way it so often is now. Parents were parents and friends were people your own age.

An example Cosby gave was that at home he was expected to get up and go to church regardless. There was no thought of sleeping in or playing games instead of attending church. Parents led their children to the house of the Lord—no excuse.

When I was young, I always thought I'd be the perfect parent. Older and wiser now, I can look back and say that if I had it to do over again, I think I'd be tougher on and more loving with my kids.

One thing I've learned is that it isn't enough for us to confide solely in God. God expects us to reach out to one another with open hearts. His love gives us the courage to love. His love covers us in joy. His love connects us and makes us want to be one—brothers and sisters and family of God. We need parents and we need friends.

After all, in relationship with God we become one in the body of Christ.

11 *Ice and Candlelight*

This week's ice storm downed trees and power lines, made for slick roads and cold homes, and disrupted school sessions and holiday shopping. The sound of the trees cracking and splintering as they crashed to the ground was intimidating enough to keep even the most adventurous inside.

We've marked time the last three days at home by the hours with power and those without. The times without were the best. Our granddaughter Gabbi spent Saturday night with us. Frightened by the lightning and thunder that signaled the storm's beginning, she sought solace in Aunt Laura's bed. Waking up to no power on Sunday, the adventure of staying warm began and with it came time to enjoy each other by playing games, talking, and laughing. David's eyes gleamed with the challenge of an icy wonderland as he headed outdoors to get cars started and the firebox filled.

Laura took pictures of the heavy tree branches that knocked over the grill and littered the backyard. She took pictures of our dog Sweetie chasing a white-tailed deer over the pond dam and the sturdy cedars so heavy with ice they bowed over the driveway.

We will send this evidence of cold times at home to Jake in the barracks of Baghdad so he can feel winter beside us.

Hard times bring out the best in us. Those without power find comfort in hotels or with family whose power is unaffected. Neighbors share hot meals with the less fortunate on their block, and bring them steaming cocoa to warm them. The able-bodied shovel ice from the widows' driveways and with their chainsaws clear trees from the road so that when all is said and done we can travel back and forth safely.

Today, I sit at work and look out at the dark sky that percolates with snow. The power is off again at home. And yet I am filled with a lightness and sense of gratitude for all God's gifts. For David, who tends to our needs. For Corey, whose love for his daughter Gabrielle shines on his face. For Laura, with whom I can discuss the inane and the prophetic. For Jake and his platoon, who defend us. For homemade bread and Christmas cookies ardently baked before the power shuts down again. For the Advent candles that light up our waiting for Jesus the Christ to be born.

During Advent, James invites us to "be patient" and "make [our] hearts firm" until "the coming of the Lord" (Jas 5:8, NABRE). Most of us experience little of the hardship the prophets endured, but merely the inconvenience of ice and candlelight now and again.

And so I pray: Dear Lord, keep me in the knowledge that all I endure is a blessing in your name. Let me always see the generosity in others and be grateful for all that you give me.

12 *My Granddaughter*

Gabbi spent the night with us on Saturday. An inquisitive soon-to-be five-year-old, she wants a play-by-play outline of our time together. I think she's preparing for a career in event planning. Can we color? Will you read to me before bedtime? Can I sleep with you? Do we have to go to church?

Invariably, the "yes" answer to the latter question brings another round of questions, ones that I never tire of answering, for they come from a child open to learning about God.

The conversation we share simply happens when we are hanging out free from deadlines, projects, or her attempts to schedule our time. This weekend she seemed concerned about good and bad people and our exchange meandered along these lines:

"Do you think God loves bad people?" Gabbi asked me.

"Yes, God loves everyone, but is sad when people choose to be bad."

"Does God love me when I do something bad?"

"Yes, God loves you just like your mom and dad do. They are disappointed in you when you choose to do bad things, but that doesn't change their love for you. That's why, when you do bad things, it's important to be sorry and apologize."

"Does God know when I'm sorry?"

"Yes, by praying you can tell God you are sorry, just like you tell anyone else."

"Is God the boss of us? Do I have to do everything he tells me?"

"God is your heavenly Father. He does not make you do what he wants, but gives you the choice to do what is good or bad."

"How can I hear God talking to me?"

"God doesn't talk to you with his voice, like you and I are talking. You know God hears you because your heart feels lighter."

With a thoughtful expression on her face, Gabbi seemed to be considering this information. Meanwhile, I, thinking this special teaching moment was at a close, started to move on mentally. What happened next amazed me. Gabbi asked me to show her how to tell God if she was sorry for something. We clasped our hands together and she repeated the few simple words I spoke that became our prayer.

What I had failed to see was that all this time, Gabbi wanted more than talk. She wanted to learn how to pray, to hear God, to know God's peace. I thought of all the Sundays spent in line for "confession," and realized that the few minutes we share with our children help form their foundation for receiving God in the sacraments. Gabbi witnessed several truths to me about sacramental preparation:

- Children thrive on routine and ritual. They may not choose going to church on their own, but quickly accept routines as part of the norm.

- Children are spiritually hungry. As little sponges, children absorb what they are taught, and do comprehend the difference between good and bad.

- Children are open to understanding. God makes sense to them in the context of a loving parent who wants us to choose good.

- Children are eager disciples. They are action-oriented, wanting practice and results. I could watch Gabbi as she tried to feel her heart being lighter after praying to God.

- Children need guidance. As parents we are blessed with the task to give our children our time, attention, wisdom, and modeling.

Therein lies the simple truth of why we practice our Catholic faith.

13 *Gifts and Talents*

Scouting out talent is the hot trend on reality television today. The viewing audience can vote for up-and-coming dancers, comedians, rock singers, and even Broadway stars, and, with text messaging, have the chance to win $10,000 for participating. At the end of the season, one new star is born, crowned, and headed for the big lights and big money.

The purpose of discovering talent at church is a bit different than on television. Christian stewardship is all about our need to give back to God for the gifts he has blessed us with. In light of this, as church leaders, our goal is to help members identify their gifts/talents, encourage their development, and use their gifts.

When we use our talents in service and praise to God, his light shines through for others to see and model. We are at our best when giving out of our strengths.

At every Mass the priest prays over the gifts that are brought to the altar. One of the prayers is, "Accept, we pray, O Lord, these offerings we make, / gathered from among your gifts to us, / and may what you grant us to celebrate devoutly here below / gain for us the prize of eternal redemption. / Through Christ our Lord."

The prayer establishes three relationships: (1) we offer our gifts to God, (2) God receives them, and (3) we seek holiness and salvation through Christ. The prayer is a communal one, embracing each of us individually and collectively. Through offertory, we are called to accept the gifts of others just as we ask Christ to accept our offerings.

Parishes that make room for members to use their gifts are welcoming and vibrant parishes. Listed below are some thoughts and recommendations on best practices from a survey of clergy, parish, and diocesan staff members and parish leaders by Parish Growth Partners:

- Parishes that scout out talents and gifts of individual parishioners and match individual interests to specific ministries are more successful.

- With active involvement comes a stronger commitment to the life of the parish and increased generosity.

- Parishes that openly and personally welcome new members and support current members see more involvement of individuals in parish activities. This is especially important in young and growing parishes.

- Initiate or renew a plan for regular recruitment of ministry volunteers.

- Initiate or renew a ministry volunteer recognition event.

- Start or reenergize a welcoming committee.

- Provide more personalized information and a direct invitation to serve.[1]

Developing and using our gifts and talents for the service and praise of God may not make us superstars, but it will make us super disciples.

Note

1. Gibson and White, *Survey of Best Practices for Parishes* (Winchester, MA: Parish Growth Partners Inc., 2006).

14 *Will He Know He Is Blessed?*

Christmas left us exhausted. The stress of hosting family and all that it entailed, the anxiousness to get back to routine amidst the desire to hold dear ones close by, the relief that came with their good-bye hugs and assurances of love—all these feelings washed over us as we took down the decorations and said good-bye to the year.

As usual, Christmas came and went with its unmet expectations, irritations, frivolity, laughter, and the joy of family reunited. The former two are forgotten after a few nights of rest, the latter three stay with us throughout life. For they reflect the joy of Advent, and it is, after all, through Advent that we know we are blessed.

Before us unfolded the familiar stories of the birth of Christ and, in his youth, being found by his parents in the temple among the teachers. At each turn, the gospels praised God and proclaimed the holiness of family. As mothers, we were warmed by the knowledge that "Mary kept all these things, reflecting on them in her heart" (Luke 2:19, 51, NABRE).

What stays in my heart this Christmas is the story of a young man thrust into adulthood unprepared. A high school student, he lives at home alone, his parents divorced and entangled in other relationships, so I am told. His mother brings groceries around and phones to check on him. He relies on his friends for transportation.

"What does he do for Christmas and other holidays?" I ask the friends who relay this sad tale. "We don't ask," they reply, accepting his situation and their inadequacy to change his course.

How will he ever know that he is blessed? I wonder. Will he ever take to heart these words of Paul?

> But when the fullness of time had come, God sent his Son, born of a woman, born under the law, to ransom those under the law, so that we might receive adoption. As proof that you are children, God sent the spirit of his Son into our hearts, crying out, "Abba, Father!" So you are no longer a slave but a child, and if a child then also an heir, through God. (Gal 4:4-7, NABRE)

As Christian teenagers and parents acquainted with this young man we wrestle with how to respond to his plight. It is difficult to adopt him, even figuratively, when our plates are full with our own families. It is difficult to erase the boundaries already built and risk interference. Does the Great Commandment to "love our neighbor as ourselves" demand more than being charitable and giving of our extra?

The answer waits at the ready: "What you do for the least of these you do for me." Not knowing this young man's heart, we are well aware that we too are the "least of these." Loving him as a son of God, an heir to the kingdom, and a neighbor requires us to accept his inherent dignity and that of his family.

It is not enough that we keep these thoughts and reflect on them in our hearts.

And so I pray: That we have the energy and compassion to reach out beyond ourselves as the Christ Child and his Holy Family call us to.

15   *Facing Mortality*

My sister Kathy called me from the emergency room Friday evening, asking me to send out prayers for her. While she was here at Christmas, Kathy was nursing a swollen ankle, thinking she had torn a ligament on one of her daily runs a couple of months before. It wasn't healing and when she got back home, she made a doctor's appointment. The ultrasound showed a blood clot behind her knee and she was rushed next door to the ER for injections of blood thinner to dissolve the clot.

Oblivious to the danger she was in, Kathy bore the pain as inconvenience and continued her routine of exercise and work as a flight attendant. How she survived with a blood clot in her leg for two months astounds her doctor. "Someone's protecting you," he told her. "If a piece of that clot loosened and went to your lungs . . ." We can imagine the rest.

Thinking about our own mortality is new to us. The six of us sisters and brothers are all in our fifties and surprised at that fact, much less of entertaining thoughts of death. But, Kathy makes it easy. Suffused with God, she long ago committed her life to his service. And she does so with a joy and energy that few can match. This brush with death, if it is that, charges Kathy's battery even more.

She knows God has called her to evangelize, to teach, to inspire. The blood clot now becomes a story, a parable to illustrate the impermanence of the body, or the preciousness of using our time wisely, or, most important, the beauty of understanding deep down that we are connected to God through the love of one another.

With the realization that we can be separated in a snap, our purpose comes clearly into focus: love. Kathy and I have staked out early morning as our time. We talk, laugh, plan, and pray, all the while treasuring the bond of love that surrounds us. I expect we have five more decades of early morning talks. Her death is not one I so readily accept or can imagine as part of my story.

And so I pray: Dear Lord, my thoughts are not of loved ones dying. I do not pray for understanding or acceptance, but for your love to carry me through the cycles of life into eternity.

16 *Culture and Youth*

The first week of January and with the New Year come our resolutions. If I were to study trends, I bet losing weight ranks number one on most lists. Television shows promise us that happiness is simply a surgery away. "Lift the eye, tighten the tummy, suck out some extra flab and your dreams will come true," advertisers lead us to believe. If going under the knife is unappealing, we can give up meat and potatoes for low-fat, low-carbohydrate prepackaged meals.

I find it funny that we visit national parks to gaze in wonder at the sequoia trees that have stood for hundreds of years, counting their rings to determine how long they have reigned. To those that have stood the longest we attribute the human traits of "wise" and "majestic."

But, when it comes to our looks, we live in the human playground that reveres youthfulness, having created cash-cow fountain-of-youth businesses that promise perfect bodies and wrinkle-free skin. I admit I am as vain as the next woman, but honestly, I have accepted that I am never going to look twenty again.

Do you think maybe, just maybe, we have taken this having baby-bottom-soft skin thing too far? One of my favorite acting couples was Jessica Tandy and Hume Cronyn. They looked real and were people I felt I could trust because their faces reflected their experiences with struggles, anguish, and joy. The fact that they had aged made them wiser, more genuine and comforting.

Sirach said it well for all times: "If you gathered nothing in your youth, / how can you find anything in your old age? / How attractive is sound judgment in the gray-haired, / and for the aged to possess good counsel! / How attractive is wisdom in the aged, / and understanding and counsel in the venerable! / Rich experience is the crown of the aged, / and their boast is the fear of the Lord" (Sir 25:3-6).

Remember the parable of the blind beggar? Jesus took pity on him and gave him back his sight. Saint John doesn't tell us that Jesus also made him younger, skinnier, or that he gave him a new body and satiny skin, merely that he cured his blindness. But many of his neighbors and others did not believe this was the same man they had always seen begging. Why? Because he was transformed by the Holy Spirit residing in him. Paradoxically, they remained blind to him, but the beggar gained sight and insight. He became a testament to Jesus Christ.

Everyone whose life Jesus touched shared that experience. The apostles and the one hundred with them in the Upper Room received the Holy Spirit after his resurrection when Jesus "opened their minds to understand the scriptures." Filled with the Holy Spirit, they were "clothed with power from on high" (Luke 24:45, 49). Their lives were forever changed. Regardless of their weight or age or looks, they became wise and loving. They shared in Jesus' command to go forth and preach the Father's love.

Imagine if we put half the time, energy, and money into seeking the Holy Spirit that we spend eradicating cellulite and loose skin. I know I could spend less time in front of the bathroom mirror and on the scale and more under the reading lamp and on my knees. I think I'll make those my permanent New Year's resolutions!

17 *Lightness*

There is lightness to the New Year, healed as we are by the brilliance of Christ's rebirth in our hearts. The Advent candles have been extinguished and the ceramic figures that enrich our images of the Christ Child's birth in the manger are lovingly stored in tissue paper and laid to rest until the season unfolds again.

Only lightness remains. A lightness that heals our insecurities, loosening the grip the dark shadows of life hold over us until they dissipate, forgotten, never to return. A lightness that allows us to radiate love; a warmth that encircles us when we give up ourselves.

You are the light of the world; Christ's words challenge us as we awaken to each new morn. By nature, daylight is the antithesis of night's darkness. Light shines on the shadow of evil, leaving it no place to hide its works of destruction.

Through the whispers of a single word, he challenges us to love: tsunami.

The stories of devastation from the Indonesian tsunami in 2004 are many—families wrenched apart by death, children left homeless, communities obliterated. Where is our God? How can we believe in lightness when thrown in the darkness of despair? There are no platitudes to ease the pain, no ointments to heal the scars already forming. Today it is the tsunami; tomorrow other sorrows will form to shatter us. We cannot bear the evil in this world.

The angel, the Holy Family, the magis are not ceramic figures to put away, but alive in each breath we take, smile we bestow, and embrace we give. We are tendrils, growing from the branch, strengthened in and by each other. We are, as they were, God's ambassadors of light in the darkness.

Evil—as is all people's—was also their foe. Herod slaughtering first-sons and causing their flight to safety, and later, disbelief turned to hatred and a call for death. Not a tsunami whose cause may be attributed to nature by some and Satan by others, but the unmistakable cruelty of man renouncing God.

"Where is our God?" we cry, weakened to our knees. "I am with you," he answers in the love we never comprehend yet always crave. With our cry, his love rushes out from the depths of our veins, nourishing every grieving tendril of our body and soul. In God, we are secure. The day does dawn and we begin anew. Healed by the light, we unfold in a love we never thought to feel again.

And so I pray: Heal us from insecurity, dear Lord, to walk in your service.

LENT

18 *Entering Lent*

Entering Lent, sacrifice is a word we are quite accustomed to hearing. But, amid the Fat Tuesday doughnuts and Mardi Gras parties, are we giving personal sacrifice much credence? Do we think of it in terms of giving up caffeine, Coors, and chocolate or are we tuned into standing beside Christ on his journey to the cross?

Sacrifice may be partially about *giving up* but in totality, sacrifice is about *surrendering*. It is less important that for six weeks out of the year we abstain from what we enjoy but, rather, that we open our hearts, minds, bodies, and souls to Christ. Our surrender to Christ continues after our Lenten diet ends, deepened by our desire to give ourselves wholly to him.

The surrendering of self brings us the joy of resurrection. What do I have of value to give Christ other than my heart to love, my mind to understand, my body to follow, and my soul to ripen in divinity? I am useless otherwise. Without surrender, the breath of life that defines me is forever silenced after my body fails. Without the empty tomb, there is no resurrection, only dust.

"Set your minds on things that are above, not on things that are on earth," St. Paul tells the Colossians (Col 3:2). His message is meant for us to abide in every day, a loving reminder that we will be raised to a life of glory with Christ.

19 *Replenished*

"Is the pond filling up?" is a question my husband David and I have been asking each other over the last few days as the rain pours down. We've been waiting for the vernacular *gully-washer*, *toad-strangler*, or *cow-soon* to saturate the earth and send water whooshing into the dry pond.

Driving across the dam this morning and seeing the water lapping against the spillway makes me smile. After three seasons with a view of sun-dried moss caked around the slope of the pond, it's a joy to have it full once again. Bring on the fishing and swimming!

Nature does provide great insight. Tooling down Highway 63 to work with the radio and cell phone off, my thoughts turn to the day's schedule at work and later to attending the evening Ash Wednesday service at our parish. A sense of blandness overcomes me and I realize I feel as dried out as the pond. Counteracting this feeling, my mind draws me into a vision of solitude and study, distant from the world.

At work, I boot up my computer to be greeted by an e-mail that links me to Pope Benedict XVI's Lenten message. My heart jumps at his phrase that references Lent as a "process of interior renewal," recognizing my own need for replenishment (Message of His Holiness Benedict XVI for Lent 2008, 1). I find myself looking forward to six weeks in the desert.

Just yesterday, my sister Kathy and I were talking about our ministries and how time for introspection is essential to us. Our conversation wound its way to the admission that knowledge without discipleship is useless; rather, the value of what we learn in solitude is in sharing it with others. The Holy Spirit feeds us through the duality of rest and service, desert and world.

I reread Pope Benedict's sentence in its fullness: "In the Lenten period, the Church makes it her duty to propose some specific tasks that accompany the faithful concretely in this process of interior renewal: these are prayer, fasting and almsgiving" (Benedict XVI 2008, 1).

The sense of blandness dissipates as I prepare to enter into Lent—both in process and tasks.

And so I pray: Dear Lord, you alone know my heart and head, their longings and thoughts. Take them as yours, in perfect union to do your will.

20 *Signs*

I believe that God prepares us for the future. Whether the upcoming events are pleasant ones or hardships to endure, I believe God bestows us with signs of his presence. Perhaps it is easier to accept God's presence as truth when we are surrounded by love, as I am fortunate to be.

Around Christmastime in 2005, our middle child Jake told us he had joined the Army and would be leaving for basic training in January. "But you've shown us no proof," I teased him, adding something like, "As far as I know you're moving to the Bahamas under an assumed name." Jake finally brought home an Army brochure meant to explain the military career to family members. His leaving was in the back of my mind throughout the holidays. Enlistment, these days, means a trip to Iraq.

Soon after New Year's, David and I were walking in the woods behind our home. We stood at the highest peak of the hillside; the trees bereft of their leaves for the winter afforded us a view that spanned several miles.

I glanced down at the earth beneath me; the dirt and dried grasses compacted under my feet. There by the toe of my shoe a rock caught my eye and I picked it up. On the summit of this common hillside, I saw the holy image of our Mother Mary in the rock. Without my prompting, David too saw the image, as did our children when we returned home.

At first, I made light of it, comparing our little find to the nonsanctioned stories of Mary seen on a burnt piece of toast or on the inside of a tunnel. Ebay here we come, I said.

By the next morning, though, I came to think of this rock as a symbol of God's presence through Mary, the intercessor. Daily prayer, I realized, is the gift I could offer to Jake as he went on to the Army. I built a small shrine around the rock, placing it in a dish on my dressing table. I leaned a prayer card of the *Memorare* and the Immaculate Heart of Mary by St. Louis de Montfort against the mirror and placed a candle beside them.

What I found is but a rock, carved by time and exposure to the elements. Where I may see the image of Mary others may not. But to me, it is a comfort, a symbol that, by offering Jake's life up to God, brings me peace. Whatever happens to Jake, I pray to be prepared.

Later that week, my eldest son Corey and I drove Jake to the recruiter's headquarters to make sure he really wasn't simply leaving us for the Bahamas.

And so I pray: As I light this candle each morning, dear Mary, I pray that you protect my son and all soldiers. Bring him home sound in mind, body, and soul. But above all, bring him to Christ. I ask this through your son, Jesus Christ, Amen.

21 *Soldier*

Months ago, I taped this saying to the bottom left-hand side of my computer monitor: "Holiness does not consist in doing extraordinary things. It consists in accepting, with a smile, whatever Jesus sends us. It is accepting, joyfully, to follow God's will" (Mother Teresa).

Last week, I affixed my son's address in Ft. Benning, Georgia, to the bottom right-hand side of the monitor, reminding me to write him a positive and cheerful note each day he's at boot camp—his one-a-day vitamin C from me.

Yesterday we received a form letter from his commander outlining the training Jake is receiving that will transform him from a civilian to a soldier. Nonchalantly tossing the letter down on the coffee table after reading it, David reassured me that "there's nothing here that Jake can't handle." He knows I need the reassurance, for we too are in the process of transforming from civilians to parents of a soldier.

Our daughter Laura's response to the letter was what I would expect from an effervescent, emotive sixteen-year-old. She respects her brother for making the decision to serve and says if he dies, it'll be doing something he believes in. Neither death nor its shadow has ever played on her doorstep.

The whole concept of my son as a soldier is a surreal one. I work for the church, for God's sake. Early on in my tenure here, someone verbalized our work as that of "soldiers for Christ." My immediate retort was that I considered myself a disciple, *not* a soldier. Disciples turn the other cheek, help the poor, and evangelize the peace of Christ. Soldiers are trained for war. What do I do now? Can I integrate the role of disciple of Christ with mother of soldier? They seem so contradictory, like Old Testament versus New Testament.

At Mass on Ash Wednesday I seek help in my confusion. Father Secrist begins with the opening prayer: "Grant, O Lord, that we may begin with holy fasting / this campaign of Christian service, / so that, as we take up battle against spiritual evils, / we may be armed with weapons of self-restraint." It dawns on me that soldiers are also trained for peacekeeping. That is a role I can accept for Jake. And, in his homily, Fr. Secrist compares Lent to spring—a time of new life, renewal, and conversion.

Jake's Lent will be spent in boot camp where he too will experience conversion. Each morning I light a candle and pray the Hail Mary for Jake's safety and acceptance into Army life. I pray he has found his vocation or will grow into his choice. I ask Mary for her intercession, to guide my son to hers, so that with each step he takes, he walks with Christ's call.

Perhaps it is all right for me to accept that my son's transformation to soldier does not necessitate my conversion from disciple to soldier. I can't begin to know the spiritual rationale that led him to the Army; rather, I find my strength as Monica praying for her son Augustine's relationship with God. Perhaps the only protection I can offer is being Jake's mother. That will have to be enough for me. Motherhood, then, leads me, as the words taped to my computer remind me, to "accepting, joyfully, to follow God's will."

And so I pray: Let these forty days be ones of reflection, acceptance of God, and ongoing growth in love.

22 *Inspiration*

I think of myself as a positive person and working in the ministry of stewardship and development suits me. I believe God is love, creation is a gift of beauty, and our faith brings us to a place of deep-seated joy.

Admittedly, in my imperfection I have many moments of falling short in loving and a few shining ones when a glimmer of God's grace pours forth from my soul. Thankfully, these next forty days of Lent give me the opportunity to cleanse myself of sin and to prepare for the glory of Christ resurrected at Easter. As bookends, Lent is the winter of our penitence and Easter the spring of our growth. Both seasons are inspirational.

Yet much of what we read and hear throughout the year emphasizes the negative, words and voices that anesthetize our thoughts of hope and joy with muck and doom. We expect this from the secular media, but, unfortunately, negativity can creep into our churches as well. And that is something we have to look out for.

After all, we claim the incredible message of eternal life and joy. I simply ask that we, as church, express ourselves in a way that matches our message, that inspires rather than exhausts.

For example, do we use the language of invitation or condemnation? Do our words emphasize how people serve instead of how they fail to serve? We seek forgiveness for our failures, but few of us are inspired by having them pointed out! Reframe the question. Instead of asking others why they are not involved, ask them where they get their energy. Use their energy in ministries that drain it and people become disheartened. Invite people to put their talents to work and they'll be on board.

Do we use the language of need or of welcome? Hearing over and over again that there are not enough volunteers in church is a question of leadership, not the quality of discipleship. If made to feel welcome, people will offer to serve in ministries they like, where they think they can achieve and will find appreciation. Simple thoughts, really, but they deserve our merit.

23 *Runaway Bunnies*

"I don't want to go to church," the two-year-old blurted out Sunday morning. "That is not a choice," said her parents, as the family was well on its way to Mass.

"Why do we go to church?" she asked. "So we can praise God," her mother patiently replied.

"Why?" the toddler persisted. "To learn to love better," her father responded with finality.

Satisfied, the child went on playing a game with her sister in the backseat and untying her shoelaces so her older sister could retie them. Once in church, the familiar took over, and the questions were forgotten.

When little ones begin attending Mass, they nuzzle up to their parents and siblings like new puppies. Infants cry when mothers get up to read. Toddlers squirm when fathers serve as ushers.

There is a magic time from elementary to middle school when kids participate willingly, wanting to sing, serve, and attend religion classes. Teens, as most parents will attest, detach from their parents in the pew and often must be dragged amid the same cries heard from the two-year-old: "I don't want to go to church." In their rush to grow up, they forget the purpose of praise and love.

The communion hymn at Ash Wednesday's service echoed God's promise of freedom to the Israelites enslaved in Egypt: "I will take you as my people, and I will be your God" (Exod 6:7). These words reverberated in my head for days. Where else had I heard them?

The rhythm of the words finally jogged my thoughts back to *Runaway Bunny*, one of my granddaughter's favorite books. The heartwarming story follows a little bunny that tells his mother he is going to run away to become a sailboat, a bird, a fish, and so forth.

Throughout the book, his mother assures him that if he becomes a sailboat, she'll be the wind that directs him; a bird, she'll be the tree he can nest in; a fish, she'll be the angler who catches him. So it goes until the bunny accepts the security of his mother's love and replies, "I might as well stay here and be your little bunny."[1]

While God promised his love and freedom to the Israelites enslaved in Egypt, many reacted with the spiritual immaturity of inquisitive two-year-olds and doubting teens. Can't you hear the incredulity of the Israelites when Moses first approached his people? "Trust God to provide for us when we have no food and shelter?" "Are you nuts, Moses? We don't want to go into the desert."

Once there, the Israelites began complaining about freedom. They wanted to return to their enslaver. They were Old Testament victims who preferred a known abuser to risking God's love and care.

We are not much different today. God continues to love and protect us, but we have such difficulty trusting and honoring him. We run from God in so many creative ways; we are slaves to our homes, jobs, status, vacation packages, and whatever else satisfies our whims.

We struggle with committing to weekly Bible studies, Mass when it conflicts with a child's sports tournament, or too much of anything spiritual that requires our consistent devotion to church or the desert.

The grace of Lent comes despite our pitiful attempts at commitment. A simple forty days to review our lives and priorities, to repent for our failures and sins, to praise God for the gift of his son's death and resurrection, and to renew our Christian vow to love one another, secure in God's promise that we are his people and he is our God.

Note

1. Margaret Wise Brown and Clement Hurd, *The Runaway Bunny* (New York: Harper & Row, 1942).

24 *Changing Expectations*

"Are we change agents or change busters?" is the question presented at Mass. Looking forward to change as an adventure or afraid of the new? Are we fenced in to sameness or free from the barriers of walls we have built around our lives?

People come and go in our lives, as do our circumstances. We change jobs, move from long-standing neighborhoods, get married, have babies, retire, add and subtract in-laws, develop new interests, face the death of loved ones. Like time, the pattern of life itself doesn't alter, only our anticipation and response do. All these thoughts encircle me, fluid as I walk through this Lenten season.

"Habit is habit, and not to be flung out of the window by any man," Mark Twain commented, "but coaxed down-stairs a step at a time."[1] Perhaps the same can be said of change, for change anticipated and prepared for can be coaxed much easier than change thrust upon us.

Recently I found an old fourth-grade textbook that I had inscribed with the following words on the inside cover: "Janie Martin is moving to Paraguay and she will be very happy."

While I cannot look back into the eyes and soul of the child who wrote this simple sentiment, I imagine anticipation and fear were present in the words, but also present was a resolution to embrace the change that I could not control.

There is still much in life I cannot control and it comes to me that to have peace and joy in my life I have to change my expectations. To do so, I ask God to narrow my span so that I may focus only on his will. For I know the choices that I make today in response to change may differ from tomorrow, as often they are temperament-based.

Flawed though it may be, a question I think we all have of God is how to grow the gifts and talents he graces us with in times when we feel locked in by change. Are we wrong in thinking the lock is there, or must we simply find the right key? Is the lock an excuse we use not to cultivate our hearts, our faith, and giving ourselves wholly to God?

I think of my mother at eighty-nine and the changes her life has taken in the last decade. As a widow, how could she know at her husband's death that she would be called to start again, to be open to new springtimes without her mate? She stays in the home she shared with my father, unwilling to fully close the door on their life to embrace a new one with us one thousand miles away. It is a lock where she finds comfort, the memories of dad present in his chair, his dresser, and his paintings on the walls. She may cling there until illness or frailty slowly removes her choices from her control. We, aware of Mark Twain's adage, continue to coax, all the while aware of how difficult it would be for us to take the paintings from our walls and close the door behind us.

And so I pray: Release me, dear Lord, from the old locks that bind me and renew my spirit.

Note

1. Mark Twain, *Pudd'nhead Wilson* (Mineola, NY: Dover, 1999).

25 *Assumption*

(Celebrating St. Mary of the Assumption Cathedral in San Francisco)

The sun rose this morning
above the cross
that held fast to the earth
and its burdens.

The light shone
like crystals in the wind,
swaying and swirling upward
in whispers of His love.

As he rose,
God grasped his right hand,
lifting him in
soft and loving touch.

Yet I, unknowing,
in distress of the sun

—my son—
sinking,
cried out against the cross,
the sorrow I accepted,
the sorrow of motherhood.

God reached down and
gently taking my left hand
loosened me from the roots
that bound me to soil and sin.

Touched again by The grace,
cleansed in the elements
of fire and water,
I wept with joy.

Darkness does not enter
this cathedral.
In fear its shadow runs,
sin dissipating among the thorns
left behind in its hurry.
The light of the east prevails.

Death does not enter
our cathedral.
We have lifted our hearts
to the Lord.
We are healed.

In the risen son
He has claimed us.
We are his.
We go and proclaim
the truth of eternal life.

26 *Lenten Peace*

Early Monday evening David and I rushed out of the house for the season's second bike ride on the trail. Having lost an hour to daylight savings time that morning, we rose out of bed bleary-eyed and grumbling, but by afternoon were ready to bolt into the warmth and light that are spring's promise.

The sun was beginning its descent into the Missouri River as we finished the last mile of our ride, and we watched its brilliant yellow turn to orange and radiate out, splashing its pink and purple hues on the water. France's great impressionists have yet to paint a more breathtaking scene.

What is it about Lent that fills me with this sense of peace I carry? Life is by no means less hectic or stressful than it was a month ago, yet I actually feel the sense of weightlessness described in the gospel song "He's Got the Whole World in His Hands." For in God's hands, our burdens evaporate.

God has given me this gift of faith, one that I surely take for granted as it has always been with me. I cannot adequately grasp or express the definition of faith. Is it the strength to follow Jesus through the hardships, to carry his cross for the sake of his great love for us; the presence of the Holy Spirit; or perhaps the hope of redemption? Lent seems the time to pray for wisdom and understanding.

For one liturgical season leads to the next. In these forty days we walk with Jesus to Golgotha, sharing the pain inherent in humankind. When we are convinced darkness will hold on forever, we rise into light with the divine Christ. At Pentecost, we receive the Holy Spirit, as Jesus foretold. God brings us an "Advocate to be with you forever. This is the Spirit of truth, whom the world cannot receive, because it neither sees him nor knows him. You know him, because he abides with you, and he will be in you" (John 14:16-17).

Faith and redemption. Though weak and imperfect, we carry God's love inside us. The Holy Spirit lives in our blood, bones, tissue, mind, heart, and soul. We nurture his presence through prayer, love of others, and obedience to his commandments.

We are blessed to live where one season leads to the next, assured that spring will turn to summer, summer to fall, fall to winter, and winter to spring. Tree branches awaken and flower, shed their leaves, and lay dormant until they bloom again. Our church parallels nature; its seasons never falter.

And so I pray: Open my heart, Lord, to fully embrace and appreciate this gift of faith.

27 *Humility*

The only true service to others comes from God. We only truly serve in God's name when we are strong enough in faith to understand our lives are gifts from God, and have an overwhelming desire to give the gift of God to others. Service is a glorious gift with which God has graced us.

As Hebrews 11:6 tells us, "And without faith it is impossible to please God, for whoever would approach him must believe that he exists and that he rewards those who seek him."

This realization does not make us haughty or proud, but humble and grateful. Wrapped in God's love, we fall to our knees in reverence and gratitude, wanting only to stay in his presence and goodness.

Mother Teresa spoke of the biggest disease of today as "the feeling of being unwanted, uncared for and deserted by everybody."[1] God gives us a yearning to love, yet so many of us feel rejected. The answer to the feeling is to venture outside us and give love to others in service to God. That is a true path to happiness.

As Catherine de Hueck Doherty expresses, "Lest the world forget about the essence of our faith, which is above all to render glory to God. The essence of our faith is to eternally seek to know God better in order to glorify him more and to serve him better in man."[2]

And Peter challenges us to serve, saying, "As each one has received a gift, use it to serve one another as good stewards of God's varied grace" (1 Pet 4:10, NABRE). It is hard for us to enact changes in our hearts until we are open to all good things, realizing God's gifts and ways come in many forms. We are so narrowly focused and single-minded that we forget to open our eyes, ears, hearts, minds, and souls to others.

We can be too self-absorbed and forget that our work is vocation—vocation that furthers God's love. If, in our personal lives, we devote our whole heart to benefit others yet in our work lives we fall short, what benefit are we as Christ's disciples? It is much easier to help others and serve as his disciples on a once-removed plane. Confronted with those in need of a friend, in need of our sympathy, in need of a friendly voice or helping hand, we oftentimes fail. In our relationships we are judgmental and confrontational. We are unsympathetic and impatient.

What I realize through Mary is that the only thing that matters is doing what is right in God's eyes, to submit my will and follow Christ without thought of reward. Too often reward is bought, purchased with acts of good done in daylight and crowds. There is no true reward there, but a vanity that does not bless God.

Or as G. K. Chesterton observed in *Orthodoxy*, "But what we suffer from today is humility in the wrong place . . . A man was meant to be doubtful about himself, but undoubting about the truth; this has been exactly reversed. Nowadays the part of a man that a man does assert is exactly the part he ought not to assert—himself. The part he doubts is exactly the part he ought not to doubt—the Divine Reason."[3]

And so I pray: Lord, share your heart with your poor servants. We have the desire to love, faith in your commitment, and knowledge of your truth, but we fail so often. Hold us and guide us, Lord, that we are truly transfigured through and in you.

Notes

1. Malcolm Muggeridge, *Something Beautiful for God: The Classic Account of Mother Teresa's Journey into Compassion* (New York: HarperOne, 1986), 73.

2. Catherine de Hueck Doherty, *Poustinia: Encountering God in Silence, Solitude and Prayer* (Combermere, ON: Madonna House, 2000), 20.

3. G. K. Chesterton, *Orthodoxy* (San Francisco: Ignatius Press, 1995), 28.

28　*Clear Stars*

Tossing in bed this morning waiting for the buzz of the alarm clock, I glanced up to a sky blanketed in thick clouds. I turned on my side and napped. Sometime later, perhaps fifteen minutes, perhaps thirty, I awoke and once again looked through the skylight cut into the roof. The clouds had been replaced by crisp, shimmering stars exploding from their inky background. Sleep let go of its hold on me and I arose to start the day with a clear mind and light heart.

My life is being rearranged. This week I welcomed my mother back to her Missouri roots, coming home after sixty years of adventures in faraway places. By her side is my sister, and with the help of many they are settling into a wonderful house and neighborhood. With the exception of a couple of years, for the larger portion of my adult life none of my family has lived in the same state, much less a hop, skip, and jump away.

Naturally I am delighted to have them nearby, yet—much to my dismay at being so shallow—I am aware it will impact my independence. I am not used to wearing the roles of daughter and sister full time.

As I weave Mom and Marilou into the fold, paradoxically I watch my son Jake depart for service in Iraq. I still don't understand my role of a soldier's mother. It is an awkward fit in that I don't want any expressions of gooey empathy from others, yet I definitely want everyone I know to pray for his safety.

Lately, the time I spend in church is dedicated to Jake. I see his life, the points of love and times we laugh about, his struggles, and, ultimately, his realization that home is his solid ground. He has bought ten acres of his own near us. The knowledge that the acreage is his tether goes unstated.

I do not understand Jake's service in the Army, and do not know if God will ever give me that insight or if he's saving it for a time (not Jake's death) when I will need or can absorb it. I do know that this week our parish is updating the prayer poster for those serving in the military. Jake's name will be present on the poster that sits below Mary's statue. I place my love under Mary's protection, light a candle, and say a novena.

The clouds that are present in my waking moments of doubt vanish with prayer. I need only behold the star that leads me to Jesus to accept and embrace life's changes with grace.

And so I pray: Dear Lord, grant me the gift of a welcoming spirit, able to embrace and let go of those I love.

29 *Time to Reflect*

It has been a cold and icy winter this year that seemed endless. But now the weather is warming, the early spring flowers are pushing their buds out from under the soil, and daylight savings begins this weekend.

Time melts away too fast—a sign that we are busy, but what does our busyness profit us? Do our works glorify God? What longing for God do we suppress in our hearts from fear of shining our light for others to see? These are questions that call to us during Lent's time of prayerful reflection.

Do we glorify God? What if we begin asking this question of ourselves as we go through each day? "Do I glorify God as I dress, eat my breakfast, pray, work, interact with others, go about the necessary errands, and live in family and among friends and community?" The question begs us to cast aside our self-limitations and give from the abundance with which God has blessed us.

God allows us to choose the path we walk in this life, though, much like the Israelites, we are discontent in the desert, opting for the green grasses of plenty instead. But God, in his infinite love, continues to provide us with spiritual manna and water, leading us "into a good and spacious land, a land flowing with milk and honey" (Exod 3:8, NABRE). We are like children, challenged to stay focused on God, from whom we receive the more valuable, the eternal reward.

As Christians, we believe that Jesus Christ is the Son of God. We believe that he died on the cross for our sins. We believe that he will come again in glory. We believe in eternal life. This is our faith.

"There is something in the depths of our being that hungers for wholeness and finality," said Thomas Merton of our journey. "Because we are made for eternal life, we are made for an act that gathers up all the powers and capacities of our being and offers them simultaneously and forever to God."[1]

Stemming from this faith, we have chosen to walk as disciples of Jesus. Lent plunks us squarely in the desert so that we may reexamine and refocus on our quest for the eternal. Easter awakens us to the joy of living in Christ and the zeal to submit ourselves in service.

And so I pray: Lord, let us recognize you as the core of our work and guide us to your ways as we continue in this path to you.

Note

1. Thomas Merton, *No Man Is an Island* (New York: Barnes & Noble Books, 2003), 140.

30　*Quality Time*

Six springs ago, when my son Jake was a high school junior, we met at a shop one afternoon to have him measured for a tuxedo for prom. A small shop, it was stuffy, crowded, and noisy, and I must admit to feeling impatient as we waited to be helped.

Sensing my discomfort, Jake reached over in his seat. Gently touching my knee, he said, "Mom, you are always talking about wanting quality time. This is quality time." He was right, and his words frequently echo back to me when I find myself forgetting to enjoy the moments I am given.

The last two months have been filled with celebrations —concerts, parties, dinners, dances, family visits—and all the ancillaries they require: phone calls, scheduling, buying cards and gifts, grocery shopping, cooking, and cleaning. There is a flurry of activity surrounding each event that seems to blend into the next. Amid all the commotion, I think back to Jake in the tuxedo shop and find the peace that comes with enjoying the events themselves.

Too many times, we expend our energy getting ready for celebrations while failing to internalize their significance. The elegance or simplicity of the event matters little. The time spent with those gathered is the important element.

Today, my friend Marilee and I met for a two-mile walk. On the one hand, our goal is to shorten our time to set a good exercise pace. On the other hand, we enjoy hanging out. Although we have never talked about it, I know she shares my sentiment that our limited time together is precious. Our walks—and the talk that goes with them—always seem to renew us. Sometimes we speak from the deepness of our hearts, but often our words are light. Deep or light, they are wrapped in the trust of a friendship well tended.

A childhood song from church wells up in me as I think about consciously making the moments spent with others special. Centered on the Eucharist, the song speaks of the joy in receiving the body and blood of Christ that fill us with the Spirit:

> We come to join in this banquet of love. Let it open our hearts and break down the fears that keep us from loving each other. May this meal truly join us as one.

If only we keep the light of the Holy Spirit alive and shining through us in all our interactions with others. If only we trust in whomever we are with and come away sated with the knowledge that we were present for each other, whether the moment was long or short. If only we were more like Christ. The song goes on to say,

> You are the son of God most high. No one can carry your name. But you came as a man, a servant, a slave, and put off your glorious power.

Christ gave himself to others as a man, a servant, and a slave. With his trust in God so complete, Christ held no fear of reaching out in the purest love. Reading the gospels, we are entranced by Christ's fullness of presence in each encounter described.

Here was a man who put aside his own needs to respond to others. Here was a man who appreciated children and recognized the marginalized. Here was a man who accepted the thanks of one leper while still healing the nine who showed no gratitude.

Knowing he was destined to a short earthly life but assured of eternal life in heaven, Christ understood quality time. Human though we are, we have that same knowledge. Use it to enjoy the gift of the little moments.

31 *Called Out of the Blue*

Susie Sly had been looking for our family for years. A friend told her about an online search engine for high school alumni and it was there that Susie found my brother Bob and sister Marilou. Bob forwarded Susie's e-mail to me last week and after some back-and-forth, she called me on Sunday to catch up.

We lived on Central Avenue in a small New York town, and the Slys lived across the street from us. They were a family with four kids, ours with six. Large families weren't that rare. The Cassidys next door had seven, the Furnesses four and that core group extended to the Manleys, Kochmans, and others whose faces I can see but whose names I have long forgotten.

At that time, sports weren't so organized that parents invested in uniforms instead of savings accounts. There was a whole neighborhood of kids to play with after school and backyards big enough to pull together an impromptu game of softball, volleyball, tag football, or whatever else we could all agree on.

We made it home in time for dinner or ran home for help if someone got hurt. (Like the time I was coming up to bat and Sally Furness, the designated umpire, was trying out her golf swing and cracked me on the head hard enough to draw blood. I swooned twice—once from the hit and the second time when hunky Mark Manley scooped me up in his arms and carried me home.) Otherwise, we were in and out of each other's yards and houses with a perfunctory holler at our moms to let them know where we were headed next.

Winters in upstate New York were cold and snowy. We went sledding in the cemetery up the hill by the ketchup factory that cast a heavy tomato smell throughout town, had snowball fights, and made snow angels.

Looking back from the vantage point of forty years, my time in Fredonia seems like a Hallmark card. Actually, it was also a time filled with the angst and drama that typifies junior high school kids living in an insulated community in the midst of a national uprising against the Vietnam War and the struggles of the civil rights movement.

The popular song was "Abraham, Martin and John," lamenting the deaths of Martin Luther King and John and Bobby Kennedy. The lyrics sung by Dion heightened the nation's sense of protest and outrage. We were too young and naive to link Abraham's death in the song with any erosion of our Christian faith or organized religion. The bloody details of King and Kennedy's deaths played out in front of us and inexorably fueled the sixties antiestablishment cry. In school, we still stood up each morning and recited our pledge to God and nation.

Sunday, when I told Susie where I work, she recalled that the first time she was in a Catholic church was with me. Susie invited me to fly in for a weekend get-together the girls have every year. "They'd be so excited to see you," she said.

I confess to having mixed emotions about going back in time. Once we've exhausted the memories we share, will there be enough common ground to hold us together? Will our laughter and friendship be renewed or will I simply be that Catholic girl that lived down the street for a while?

And so I pray: Dear Lord, these forty years hence I find myself settled. Give me the courage to risk bridging the past with the present.

32 *Flexing for Christ*

Coming off a full weekend of hosting a financial seminar, our annual stewardship retreat, and attending a vocations confirmation day, this morning my sister Marilou commented that she now understands why I don't plan meals ahead of time. Mind you, I am an excellent planner when it comes to work, trips, events, and the like. But don't ask me on Wednesday what we're going to have for dinner on Sunday. It's inconsequential when I am simply trying to stay on target with what today brings. First things first could be my motto.

In Stephen Covey's book by the same name, he speaks of getting the most out of life, using the visual of filling a container by putting in the big rocks first, then adding sand and then water. "The objective," Covey says, "is not to fill the container to the brim, but to make sure that the big rocks are there and that the container is not so full it can't accommodate conscience-directed change."[1]

Children, family, and work are my big rocks. I lay those at the feet of the Rock—my Christ, my church, my faith. Instead of considering my relationship with Christ as one of the rocks in my container, I think of it more as the one truth that underlies all that is important to me. I am here to serve Christ through my children, family, work, and whatever else Christ brings my way.

Keeping room for Christ to redirect us, or "conscience-directed change," as Covey calls it, requires the art of flexibility and not a little juggling. Oftentimes, to respond to the opportunities Christ brings our way, we have to accommodate or throw out our schedule. Serving as a communion minister at the evening Mass may mean meeting friends later than we planned. Babysitting our grandchildren may mean we give up our evening out. Having an open-door policy for our children's friends may mean a loss of privacy, sleep, and a stocked refrigerator! We serve Christ in many simple ways every day, and each one requires our flexibility. Flex(ibility) for Christ—what a great motto!

Messing with our schedules may be only the beginning of what Christ has planned for our lives. He makes his move in our hearts, bit by bit prying them open to reveal the gifts planted within us for his service.

Ultimately, it is up to us to say, "Yes, dear Jesus, shake up my life."

And so I pray: Dear Lord, keep my door always open, keep my schedule in pencil, and fill my container with the joy of doing your work.

Note

1. Stephen Covey, A. Roger Merrill, and Rebecca R. Merrill, *First Things First: To Live, to Love, to Learn, to Leave a Legacy* (New York: Simon & Schuster, 1994), 161.

33 Steady in Christ

It amazes me to think how Jesus came to the apostles to make real his promise of rising again yet always being among them. The apostles, who were afraid and helpless, whose spirits sank low after Jesus' death, received the pure and everlasting energy of the Holy Spirit that allowed them to recommit to God for life, to preach, to heal. People standing under their shadow were cured! Wow.

No wonder Paul reminded Timothy to "stir into flame the gift of God that you have through the imposition of my hands. For God did not give us a spirit of cowardice but rather of power and love and self-control" (2 Tim 1:6-7, NABRE).

If these incredible gifts were given to twelve who turned away while having Jesus present in body with them, then we can appreciate Christ giving the spirit of power, love, and self-discipline to those who believe and trust in him even though we have not experienced the physical man of two thousand years ago.

We have the risen Christ, the divine, the all-encompassing lover, the Spirit within who gently continues to open our hearts to receive others. We are so indebted to Christ, mere branches on the vine, tenuously blown about by the breeze and knowing more and more that we must cling tenaciously to him as the food that keeps us nourished and well-rooted in truth.

For in times of exhaustion, fear, and helplessness it is easy to wander. What bears remembering is that Christ is always true to believers. He does not respond like a mortal man. Though in his weakness Peter denied Jesus, Christ did not punish Peter for his lack of trust or give him less sheep to feed or otherwise cast him aside. Christ lovingly lifted him from his fall. Christ recognized the faith and purity of Peter's heart and assigned him with the monumental task of building the church. Christ reenergized him.

And so I pray: Lord, keep a firm grip on us as the waves of life swirl around us, that we may stay steady in our faith and service to you.

34 *Walking Together*

My sister Kathy and I keep trying to get together. She lives out on the West Coast in California, and I have yet to visit her in the new condo she moved into, though she's lived there going on five years. We are prayer partners, she and I, phoning each other several times a week and e-mailing about the same. Each phone call ends the same, with my "I love you," and Kathy's response, "I love you more." Being the elder by a year and four days, she always gets the final word! We hang up amid laughter and smiles.

She has that big personality; she's the person who brings a smile to your face and warmth to your heart every time you see, hear, or think of her.

As children we were always close. As adults walking together in Christ we are even closer. In our youth we shared a bedroom and exchanged clothes. Now we are separated by thousands of miles yet come together in prayer. We are bound by blood, the blood of kinship and Christ. Kathy and I experience the promise of the Holy Spirit: "For where two or three are gathered together in my name, there am I in the midst of them" (Matt 18:20, NABRE).

God created us with this marvelous nature of seeking companionship, intending us to walk alongside one another through life in a community of faith. We are not meant to live on personal islands removed from the body of Christ. "Spirituality is not a private search for what is highest in oneself but a communal search for the face of God," says Rev. Ronald Rolheiser.[1]

When we worship with our faith community, we celebrate and give testimony to the birth, life, death, and rising of Jesus Christ. We receive the body and blood of the one who will love us through this life and into eternal life. We proclaim our faith as one body of Christ. We strengthen each other to follow Christ, to be his disciples and to serve others. Baptized, we are daughters of Mary, sisters of Christ, and children of God. We are automatically members of the Christian community and tied to one another. God gave us life for a purpose. Being present in community joins us with others to fulfill that purpose together.

Phone calls and e-mails are not enough. It is time I visit Kathy in her condo.

And so I pray: I am one of many in this community of God. So blessed to be loved, to be among the holy. Just that drop of water on my brow and I am saved from sin. Your healing oil so tenderly applied. Your loving word, so gently spoken. Our voices raised in praise to the one true God. Such joy. Unworthy, yet healed.

Note

1. Ronald Rolheiser, *The Holy Longing: The Search for a Christian Spirituality* (New York: Doubleday, 1999), 69.

EASTER

35 *Easter Joy*

This Holy Week we walk with the disciples as they eat the Last Supper, see their master taken from the Garden of Gethsemane and hung on a cross, and experience the joy of his resurrection. Easter Sunday, the church bells ring with the joy of the Risen Christ. For Christ's resurrection has secured our eternal life.

When we choose to live in a state of joy—as much as is possible in a broken world where we also experience tears, heartache, and suffering—we are sanctified to receive the pure joy of heaven. Think of the difference between our spiritual lives in heaven versus on earth. On earth we bake with vanilla extract; in heaven everything is pure vanilla made from the richest beans!

To live in joy means to love indiscriminately. To love thus means forgiveness is key. Often, when we think of heaven, we put it in the context of meeting all our desires:

Heaven is the best fishing spot where the big ones don't get away.

Heaven is a wall-to-wall shopping mall where I can get everything in abundance.

Heaven is a library with all the great books on its shelves.

Heaven is filled with pastries that I can eat and never gain weight!

You get the idea.

But if joy is pure love and heaven is the perfection of joy, does that define heaven as the state or place where our earthly desires are granted?

In his book *Happiness: Lessons from a New Science*, British economist Richard Layard notes that some factors affecting our happiness are external ones, while others "work from inside us, from our inner life." Further, he indicates that studies show "people who believe in God are happier."[1]

Joy is the long-term result of not compromising our faith for temporal success.

The joy-filled people I know do not bear lesser burdens than others do. They bear them easier by giving them up to God. They do not suffer less sorrow, but suffer it more sweetly in faith. They understand the spiritual meaning of being tested by fire.

They live the words of Nehemiah, who said, "rejoicing in the Lord is your strength!" (Neh 8:10, NABRE). Having experienced joy, they choose to let go of bitterness and the pain it brings. They embrace the gift of life's struggles. They bounce back.

Life on earth is simply a short test, preparation ground for the cool breezes and sunny days that define eternity. Naively, perhaps, I think how easy it is to believe in life united with God. I have no magic words that can make a difference, only a silent prayer. For God gave each of us the gift of free will.

And so I pray: Dear Lord, help me to experience and reflect the Easter joy Jesus gave me as gift through his resurrection.

Note

1. Richard Layard, *Happiness: Lessons from a New Science* (New York: Penguin, 2005), 6, 72.

36 *Fear and Love*

"We have nothing to fear but fear itself," said FDR in 1933. In this time of war and global vulnerability that statement sounds trite. Some are afraid the end time is near. For many others, war is in our thoughts as we change routines to avoid places we would have usually gone, events we would have unquestionably attended. Rather than living normally, we become immobilized by fear. Indeed, our paralysis reflects FDR's subtle message to, above all, fear the unlived life.

It is naive to think we can vanquish fear or the threat or actuality of war. It is true that we are born, we live, and we will die. Our challenge is how we choose to live. God gives us this precious gift of life on earth not to claim as our own but to further God's eternal kingdom. In the short life span of our hometown United States of America, God has endowed us with many freedoms: to learn, to express ideas, to work, and to worship.

To preserve these freedoms we must first recognize God as their source. Freedom is not reading only to understand the words, speaking only for the debate, or working merely for financial gain. Freedom is giving all of ourselves to God, submitting our wills to God's great plan. To worship we must open our hearts to the Father. We must seek his direction through prayer, acknowledging our limitations as human servants of the perfect Christ.

As stewards of God's gifts of life and freedom, we are called to action regardless of circumstance. As St. Hilary said, "I am well aware, almighty God and Father, that in my life I owe you a most particular duty. It is to make my every thought and word speak of you."[1]

Whatever talent or duty God bestows on us is merely self-gratifying until we hear his call. When our hearts long to do God's will, we can set aside complacency despite fear, responding in the affirmative with full faith that where God takes us, he gives us the words to speak, the bread to eat, the place to rest.

Saint Benedict is an exemplary role model for stewardship in action. Forsaking the temporal pleasures of the world, he became abbot and founder of the Benedictine Order. In the Rule of Benedict, the early Christian set forth the standard for life in monastic communities and ideals for Christian spirituality that still endure. Under the four tenets of prayer, study, labor, and community he advised, "With his good gifts which are in us, we must obey [serve] him" (RB Prol. 6).[2]

Contrasting other monastic groups around 500–540 AD, St. Benedict's communities flourished with his commonsense instructions encouraging the perfection and use of individual talents for the good of all. The firstfruits harvested through Benedictine labor were witnessed in the education of youth, building of cathedrals, and flourishing of scholarly writings.

Since recorded time, the world has not seen a century of peace. Conflict seems to reside hand in hand with humankind, whether in our neighborhoods or far-off continents. Yet, Christ's message of love and hope and stewardship has never faltered. Our earthly lives may not always be filled with ease, but we hold the choice of ongoing spiritual joy in God.

We need simply to engage.

Notes

1. Saint Hilary of Poitiers, Liturgy of the Hours, vol. III (New York: Catholic Book Publishing, 1976), 1301.

2. Rule of Saint Benedict 1980, ed. Timothy Fry (Collegeville, MN: Liturgical Press, 1981).

37 *Apostolates and Ministries*

I was surprised to find the five-hour drive to Wichita relaxing and energizing. Despite the forecast, I ran into little rain; it came in one-minute spurts every now and then, with the sole effect of keeping the outside of the car clean. Flint hills were the scenery the last ninety miles from Emporia. No malls, concrete, houses, Starbucks, or other signs of urban life; simply gentle hills of pebbles yet to spark with the greening effect of spring. God's presence filled me with peace.

Our meeting was held last Friday at the Spiritual Life Center in Wichita, where we could retreat from radio and television, celebrate Mass, and stay focused on our common purpose. As stewardship directors representing fifteen dioceses from four states, we gather two to three times per year to help one another in our work to empower Catholics to live discipleship as Christian stewards. Working together for seven years now, we are a close-knit group. I am always left humbled by the spirituality, knowledge, and genuine caring so freely offered by my peers. We know we are blessed.

Bishop Jackals opened Saturday's diocesan stewardship conference that followed the previous day's regional meeting. In a clear and organized manner, he spoke to the 240 of us gathered in the sanctuary about our roles in serving the mission of the church. Lay ministers are called to collaborate between the *apostolate* and *ministry*, he explained. The lay apostolate "illuminates and orders temporal affairs according to the plan of God, bringing the light of Christ into all places." The lay ministry is "ordered to the needs of the church to build it up from within and work under the leadership of the pastor." Serving as apostles, we take Christ into the community and as ministers we strengthen the church.

The five-hour ride home gave me time to think about his words. Stewardship's premise is that everything we are and have—even our lives—is gift from God. Our talents and how we return them to God are expressed in our choice of vocations. They who answer God's call to the priesthood serve through distinct roles, to sanctify, tend, and govern. Why, I thought, do we cry out for bits and pieces of priestly roles to be given to us when we have chosen to serve God as laity? It occurred to me that in so doing we denigrate the holiness inherent in all roles.

This small moment of grace affords me the realization that I am blessed to serve God in whatever manner he chooses to call me.

On our evening walk yesterday, David and I picked one of every wildflower we saw blooming: Dutchman's britches, sumac, violet, Jack-in-the-pulpit, an array of white, yellow, purple, and deep burgundy. I presented them to Laura and asked her to take a picture of them for my computer's screen saver. The season fades too quickly and I find myself wanting the visual proof to remind me of the beauty of new life and the promise of its rising again and again.

The asparagus is not ready to pick. It's peeking out of the dirt enough to tease us, but we know with warmer weather coming, we'll soon be bent over the rows every evening snapping the tender spears. There won't be time for leisurely walks. What were we thinking by planting four more rows last spring? Certainly not about our backs. Yet the physical motion of walking down to the patches to pick, filling the bags, spreading our yield onto the maple island, weighing it and bundling it, offer me a contentment that is hard to describe. Much like the flint hills and the wildflowers, farming offers me a mental quiet that allows me to hear God and roots me in gratitude for the goodness of his land.

38   *Sophie's Diamond*

"May I please have a few more flat-rate boxes?" I asked the clerk at the post office on Holy Saturday. She taped the customs form to the package I was mailing to Jake and handed me the receipt and three boxes. Walking out to the car, I realized with great elation that the boxes I held signified the last three shipments I'd be making to Jake at his APO address.

He is scheduled to leave Iraq from the Baghdad International Airport on or about May 5—give or take a few days depending on how the planes are running—returning to his base in Ft. Benning, Georgia, for debriefing before receiving thirty days' leave. As you can imagine, we are counting down the days. And so is Sarah, his fiancée. The two are making the most of Jake's homecoming; they are getting married here on June 7!

Rings were one of the wedding subjects we chatted about around the kitchen table Easter Sunday. Several years ago, Mom had given me her mother's diamond ring and with it a slice of family history to treasure. I recounted the facts of the story Mom has told me since childhood, adding my own impressions and images that have grown in its retelling.

The ring had originally belonged to my great grandmother Sophie, a gift from her husband, my great grandfather, Herschel Nichols. The couple raised their family in the small town of New Bloomfield, where Herschel made his living as publisher of the town's newspaper.

I can imagine Sophie sitting down to rest at day's end, chores completed and kids in bed, absentmindedly twirling the ring around on her finger, then stretching out her hand to look at the sparkling diamond, as I do now a century later. Then, on an evening of hundreds like it, Sophie stretched out her hand to find the diamond missing from its setting.

In a panic, she called out to Herschel. A man of action, he took the lantern down from its hook and went out in the dark of night to look for the diamond. It had rained that day and the ground was wet. The air was mild and a soft breeze lifted his spirit. He shone the lantern in the muddy tracks made by the wagon wheels, whistling as he meandered down the lane in front of their house.

While not expecting to find the diamond, nonetheless Herschel was enjoying the fresh air and kept swinging the lantern back and forth, somewhat distracted with thoughts of tomorrow's news left to write and have arranged on wooden blocks for printing.

How surprised Herschel must have been when the light shining in the mud winked back. Keeping his eye on the shiny object, he set down the lantern, and bent over to pick it up. A smile formed around his lips when Herschel drew the object to the light and saw Sophie's diamond sparkling between his fingers.

"Ah," we all sighed to hear our hopes were confirmed. The ring entrusted to me is set with the original stone—Sophie's diamond. One day I will have the pleasure of taking it off my finger and handing it down to Laura. Until it's her turn to pass it on, Laura will wear the ring and preserve our family story of the day Sophie lost her diamond and Herschel found it in the muddy tracks made by the wagon wheels.

And so I pray: I come to you with praise and thanksgiving, Lord, for the stories of old that bind us as family to our ancestors and common heritage. May Jake and Sarah treasure their pasts and bind them together with their story.

39 *Not Fearing*

Driving on the highway to work this morning, I laughed when I saw the "No Fear" sticker on the back of a truck that passed me. Recently at dinner we were teasing our son Corey about having that sticker on the 1971 restored Chevy Cheyenne truck he bought for himself in high school. He did look cool riding around in that classic black truck! Teenagers—as do we all—get sucked in by marketing all the time.

No Fear is a company that sells clothing and other products to fans of the motocross industry. It's positioned to "rebel against the profit-hungry trends of their competitors," said Britt Galland, former vice president of marketing, on its website. "We're a different company, so people have to get over their ideas of who they think we are." The message he not so subtly conveyed is that this company (1) caters to the rebel in us and (2) is against being labeled.

As rebels we visualize the high speeds, roar of the crowd, feel of the great outdoors, thrill of the race, celebrating wins and bemoaning losses with friends.

Letting our minds float out the office window we think, "Ah, what freedom! Can life get any better than that?"

Paradoxically, the company that wants to stand apart from any greedy corporate label makes its profit from a label. Mind you, I'm not dissing No Fear; I kind of admire the company's cleverness. It's carved out a niche by tapping into our longings to be forever daring and—most likely as the founders age—forever young.

In reality, most of us are spectators rather than rebels. Now and again we may tire of our routine and daydream about escape from the ties that bind, whatever they may be. But, when we peel off the emotional veneer that defines marketing and place ourselves in God's hands instead, we discover the great gift of trust.

Trust requires no sticker, no t-shirt, no expensive vacation, no stuff. Trust is rebellious, bubbling up despite gloomy economics or discouraging news. Trust can't be labeled because it resides in the depths of love and shows itself in uncanny ways. "I sought the LORD, and he answered me, / delivered me from all my fears," says the psalmist (Ps 34:5, NABRE). Trust.

Now an adult, Corey has long since outgrown No Fear stickers. His current Chevy truck sports his company logo! We are proud parents of an entrepreneur who embodies a value that makes America great—the freedom to schedule his own eighty-hour workweek!

And so I pray: Dear Lord, take from me any desire to have no fear and replace it with a genuine trust in your presence. Therein lies my freedom.

40 *Riding It Out*

Something's wrong. Since April 1 I have diligently watched for the signs of spring. I savor every aspect of the season, from the wildflowers popping, grass greening, trees budding, turning off the heat, to opening the windows and letting the fresh air cleanse the house. Every year I remind myself to slow down and enjoy the beauty of nature rising. But now I cry out, "Just get me through the next two months, Lord!"

Corey has two homes on the market and is busy building more. Jake is coming home from Baghdad, getting married, and returning to Ft. Benning, Georgia, with his bride. Laura is being confirmed and graduating from high school to head for college in the fall. We are delighted with the joy they find in life and proud of their accomplishments.

But, I have to admit that I feel a bit like Jimmy Stewart in *It's a Wonderful Life*, restlessly watching my children flying off to experience life on their own while David and I receive quarterly social security notices apprising us of how much we'll receive if we retire in twelve or twenty years. Is there no adventure left for us?

Are these bittersweet stirrings symptoms of the dreaded empty nest syndrome? Are there stages one experiences such as in death and divorce? Are there guidelines to walk us through the feelings of listlessness and anxiety (root cause: not waiting up for a teen to come home), to euphoria mixed with puzzlement (root cause: we're free but what do we do now?), to contentment (ah, peace and quiet!)?

The thing is, we really aren't free nor do we want to be. While they may not realize or acknowledge it yet, our kids are as rooted in us as we are in them. They may think our ideas are outdated, or our advice isn't always to their preference, but we are their solid ground. As such, we can't afford to be trapped by *any* syndrome, no matter how psychologically categorized, justified, or deserved.

I find myself thinking of all the possibilities awaiting me now that my obligations of raising children are waning. "Take time before making any major changes," I have counseled others going through life's ups and downs. "Ride it out," I now tell myself. "Read, exercise, play more."

Last fall, friends gave us a gift card for a weekend at a bed-and-breakfast in Hermann. Sometime in July we're putting our bikes in the back of the truck and going for a ride. Who says we aren't adventurous?

And so I pray: Let my heart always be open to your calling, oh God. Let my ears hear and my will be firmly planted in your way.

41 *Confirmation*

My sister Kathy and I received the sacrament of confirmation in third and second grades, respectively, during the same Mass at which we received our first Holy Communion. I don't remember the patron saint Kathy chose for her confirmation name, but I chose St. Thérèse of Lisieux, the Little Flower. She was a popular saint during my childhood.

We dressed in floor-length white dresses, carried little white Bibles in our white-gloved hands, and wore "mantillas" to cover our heads. And, in keeping with the style of the time, we wore shiny black patent leather shoes! I still have the picture taken of us smiling and squinting in front of the banana tree in our backyard. As kids, Kathy and I could have passed for twins.

Kathy remembers me being nervous at Mass and seeking her guidance to kneel at the proper times and correctly follow all that we were taught in class. While the ceremony has faded into memories and pictures, its impact on our lives remains strong. In our own ways and vocations (however humble their effect) we have chosen to serve Christ as his disciples.

Confirmation calls us precisely to that point. Through the anointing of the chrism oil and the laying on of hands, we have been "sealed with the Gift of the Holy Spirit" and "assume the role of disciple and witness to Christ."[1]Last Friday we celebrated at the "An Evening with the Bishop" dinner and auction to support vocations. As our Bishop John R. Gaydos spoke about our efforts to encourage vocations, it occurred to me that I was sitting in a room with six hundred disciples. Farmers, bankers, merchants, parents, teachers, artists—all breaking bread together— present to listen, visit, and support vocations. What stories, I wonder, do each of those gathered have to share with their children or friends? Do they realize how the holiness of their daily walk impacts those who are searching for their vocations?

This year, Bishop Gaydos will confirm hundreds of young and older adults throughout our diocese. In the next few weeks he will anoint my daughter Laura with the chrism oil and, laying his hand on her head, will mark her with the seal of the Holy Spirit.

Belonging to Christ, Laura has chosen St. Genevieve to guide, strengthen, and walk with her on her path of discipleship.

And so I pray: Dear Lord, may Laura recognize your ever-presence and meet the joys and challenges of this life as your disciple.

Note

1. *Catechism of the Catholic Church*, 2nd ed. (Vatican City: Libreria Editrice Vaticana, 1994), 1320, 1319.

ORDINARY TIME

42 *Stillness*

Stillness surrounds me this morning. I feel it in the release of tension in my neck and shoulders. I absorb it in the soft pink light of dawn that reflects off the pond. Except for the ambient noises the appliances make, the house is quiet—no wind to stir up the chimes or footsteps treading on the floor.

I do not distract myself with thought or action or otherwise disturb the stillness; for in the calm I become aware of God's presence. The prayer of praise surrounds me and emanates from within me. God is the match and the flame; the spark and the warmth it creates.

"I am," he tells us, beyond the external influences of time and matter that we associate with our span of life. "God is love, and whoever remains in love remains in God and God in him," the apostle's letter reminds us (1 John 4:16, NABRE).

In *The Power of Now*, Eckhart Tolle asks us to consider that "the moment your attention turns to the Now, you feel a presence, a stillness, a peace. You no longer depend on the future for fulfillment and satisfaction—you don't look to it for salvation. Therefore, you are not attached to the results. Neither failure nor success has the power to change your inner state of Being. You have found the life underneath your life situation."[1]

Apart from God, nothing I think, feel, sense, or own is meaningful. The world may place value on knowledge, desires, and wealth, but these are false without God. If, in his intellect, G. K. Chesterton had not accepted God, the soul of his writings would be lost and only his witticism would survive in shallowness. If we pursue our hearts' desires without God, even those meant for the good of others, our self-gratification in their accomplishment would be short-lived, replaced by the malaise of emptiness. If oil dries up, stock markets plummet, and economies collapse, God will be the same "I am."

I will continue to mark the light and dark of days and nights, dates in this new year's calendar, and the seasons nature provides. All the while, I will seek the stillness, the presence of God wherein my life and love abide.

And so I pray: Dear God, let me recognize you as love and find your presence within me. Let me strip away the external and find myself as your love. Let your love emanate from me to my neighbor.

Note

1. Eckhart Tolle, *The Power of Now: A Guide to Spiritual Enlightenment* (Novato, CA: New World Library, 2004), 68–69.

43 *Stewardship*

I've just returned from the annual International Catholic Stewardship Council conference. Conferences are a funny thing. Once working in a professional field for a few years, we claim to attend them simply to pick up a kernel of information, obviously knowing an abundance about our subject matter already. However, I discovered that knowledge comes in many forms, that by emptying my preconceived notions to listen to God's will I gained insight into stewardship heretofore gone untapped.

As a child, I attended a Peruvian classroom at the all-girls' Catholic school of Villa Maria in Lima. Of the fifty-four girls in my class, I was the only Norteamericana. All our textbooks were in Spanish. We spoke, read, wrote, and played in Spanish. As a result, I was imbued with the Spanish language and culture from the age of two, and, for all purposes, I was raised a Latina. My command of the language came naturally without effort.

Yet, here I am, a forty-something woman still crawling in my knowledge of stewardship as a way of life. With effort, I am learning what it means to be a mature disciple of Christ. My husband and I have raised two sons into adulthood, and have a daughter still on her way. We've supported them at countless basketball, baseball, soccer, football, and swimming events; concerts, marching band, boy scouts, girl scouts, 4-H, homework, flus and ear infections. Wrapped around years of activities and events, church has served as our spiritual home.

It dawns on me that we walk hand in hand with stewardship in all we teach our children from birth. Stewardship is as natural as our intake and expulsion of breath. Stewardship is ingrained in me just like my childhood fluency in Spanish. But, like language, stewardship grows rusty without constant use. Until we appreciate that each aspect of our life is God-given, our stewardship lies dormant.

The bishops' Pastoral Letter on Stewardship (2002) defines these sentiments through three underlying convictions:

- Mature disciples make a conscious, firm decision, carried out in action, to be followers of Jesus Christ no matter the cost to themselves.

- Beginning in conversion, change of mind and heart, this commitment is expressed not in a single action, nor even in a number of actions over a period of time, but in an entire way of life. It means committing one's very self to the Lord.

- Stewardship is an expression of discipleship, with the power to change how we understand and live out our lives.

As disciples, we respond to these convictions in four ways: we recognize that God is the source of all that we have; he has made us stewards or caretakers of his gifts; we are grateful for these gifts; and we share them generously in love of God and others.

Yes, we've heard these words before. But we gain more than a kernel of information by opening our hearts to receive their pure meaning and practice that meaning in our lives.

44 *Giving*

We are here as faithful stewards because God has tapped us on our shoulders. We seek life with him on a higher plane, on a spiritual dimension beyond materialism. We seek

- connections and relationships with each other in a spiritual community,
- to be understood, and
- fulfillment of our human potential through God.

But, because we are so grounded in our society and its culture, oftentimes it is easier to ignore God's tap, or to say, "Not right now, Lord, I'm much too busy or weak or unable to serve." Yet, God keeps on tapping our shoulders.

Sometimes, God taps us for years, working in areas we are afraid to address, before we finally wear down and say yes. Once we say, "I'm ready, Lord," and make that commitment, we climb another step closer to God, to peace, to life on a spiritual dimension. We realize the fears that hold us back are rooted in our lack of faith.

And that one little yes, that one little commitment, strengthens us beyond words, allowing us to grow even closer to God and each other.

When I moved to Missouri almost twenty years ago, God began tapping me on the shoulder about stewardship. (At least, that is when I was ready to acknowledge the tapping!) I began giving of my time and talent, but treasure is much harder.

My habit during offertory was to give whatever I thought I could afford that week, whatever was left over. At the time, as a single mother with two children, there was never much left over. Looking back, I realize my gifts were also emotionally based. Sometimes I gave $1 and sometimes I gave $5. If the pastor's homily especially challenged or moved me, I gave more.

If I really needed God's help that week, I gave more. I was missing the point of stewardship! My giving was not based on faith in God; rather, it was based on an impulsive view of my own needs.

As I began listening more to God, I realized that to be a steward I had to take a risk and give to him first, that my giving needed to be budgeted and intentional. Oftentimes our struggles with tithing are a reflection of our society and the wish-list mentality it imposes on us. While tithing should be a sacrifice, rather than our leftover change, I think it is detrimental to picture *what* we have to *give up* in order to tithe sacrificially.

Vacation.

New big-screen TV.

Car.

Whatever is on our current wish list.

Why? Because we wind up equating God and his community with material things. Sadly, we weigh our momentary desires in making the decision about whether or not or how much to tithe.

Jesus clearly tells us that tithing is an act of faith that blesses us tenfold. In making a commitment to our community we walk closer to Jesus and to each other. We reap far more than the material toys with which society seduces us. We gain life on the spiritual plane, growing in faith through each challenge God presents.

In our society, we do not really trust God to take care of us. Rather, we espouse taking care of ourselves. While an essential ingredient in sound financial management is securing our future needs, the danger in this philosophy is that we may lose sight of being our brothers' and sisters' keepers. We may see our elderly, our poor, our broken and think, "They should have taken care of themselves."

The most important belief we can pass on to our children is our faith in God and the knowledge that we are our brothers' and sisters' keepers. If we do not clearly establish these fundamental principles through our own actions, who will teach them to our children?

I believe we must invest in God first—his stock market will never crash!

God has tapped us all on our shoulders. Yet making the decision to commit to God and our community is a difficult one. We feel a tremendous sense of risk in doing so. Let us ask for God's guidance in prayer.

And so I pray: Dear Lord, we come to you as a community asking that you open our minds and our hearts, giving us courage to respond to your tap on the shoulder. Help us to grow spiritually and to live in faith with you.

45 *Mexico*

Ah México, una gente acogedora a pesar de su situación económica. Oh, Mexico, a welcoming people despite their economic climate. Walking through Cozumel's downtown away from the tourist shops catering to the cruise ships, my sister and I sought the soul of the city.

Away from the carefully guarded white beaches and glitz, their sidewalks are in poor shape. Weeds push up the concrete and walking sight unseen becomes a perilous adventure. Water lies in the streets mingled with old paint chipping from rundown buildings.

In the center of town, there is no planned zoning, no green space between buildings, but wrought-iron fences to separate homes from the shops that are lined up in colorful rows beside each other. There are no neon signs or shopping mall parking spaces. Instead, people walk in and out of stores and down the streets attending to their daily business.

We walk for blocks and blocks, looking for Don Raul and the Talavera tile we hope he carries. Along the way, we get directions that point to the steeple of the Catholic church as our landmark.

"Turn left past the church and his shop is just a half block up," she leads us in Spanish. When we arrive and introduce ourselves to Don Raul, he tells us his son handles the tile portion of the family's furniture store. Regretfully, he is not available now, but was called home to tend to his son who has a fever. "I cannot help you," he iterates, "the tile is his job." In Mexico, we are delighted to learn, money—with an exchange rate of ten pesos (cents) to the US dollar—does not reign over devotion to family or respect for others' position.

Don Raul recommends another shop. His directional landmark is the *escuela Catolica*—the Catholic elementary school. Reaching the school, we first notice its shabbiness. Then we see the kids streaming outside, going home for their noon meal, we guess.

Watching a young girl wearing her white oxford shirt and red and navy skirt fills me with a sense of home. She wears the same uniform as my daughter. A thousand miles away from our hometown of Columbia, Missouri, in a country designated as poor by the world's standard, she bounds out of school laughing and chatting with friends as mine does, waiting to be picked up.

As we stand across the street enthralled at this scene, a man arrives riding an old bicycle with a mini-trailer on wheels attached to its front. He is hauling a four-drawer dresser. The young girl smiles at her papa, climbs aboard, and sits cross-legged on the cardboard floor of the trailer with her back leaning against the dresser.

I visualize my daughter being picked up in her father's work truck with its landscape machinery stowed in the trailer on back. Ready to be traded in, not too far in the future we figure, the truck boasts large roomy seats, heating and air conditioning, a CD player, and full power. Not quite the same as this papa's and his niña's ride home.

Approaching the father, I explain that I too have a young daughter and wish to show her the commonality of faith and dress that our girls share. We shake hands and they graciously pose for a picture.

We walk on, finding the little open-air shop where I buy the decorative ceramic tile and cross for our front door that will serve as reminders of my childhood as a gringa/Latina living overseas. My God, my sister and I realize, we are so blessed to be among a people so warm and welcoming.

And so I pray: Dear Lord, let us continue to welcome the stranger among us as we have been loved.

46 *Thanks*

In front of our house sits a small pond where in warm weather we enjoy swimming and fishing. But in the winter it is transformed into a treacherous obstacle we must avoid, as the driveway around the pond serves as our only access to the main road. This past winter, with the ice frozen thickly on the ground, my daughter and I got in the habit of buckling our seat belts, holding hands in prayer, and asking God to keep us safe as we anxiously skirted the pond and headed to work and school.

Winter melted into spring, and the habit has stayed with us, the thanks and supplication of prayer becoming an expectant part of our morning routine. It tickles me to realize that we are giving our first please and thank you of the day to God.

Last weekend I took part in a stewardship retreat with clergy, religious, and laypeople representing several churches and towns. Stewardship is defined as the realization that everything we have is a gift from God. We are but stewards, or managers, of these gifts. We are called to accept our gifts with gratitude, to share them with others, and to return them with increase to God.

In his homily at the retreat Mass, Bishop Gaydos spoke of stewardship as living *in* Christ, explaining that giving our hearts to Christ changes the tension in our daily lives from disabling to creative. "Our external circumstances don't necessarily change, but our anxiousness dissolves," he said. The simple truth of that statement touches me with a joy that parallels the relief I feel making it safely across the pond on icy winter mornings.

Living in Christ, we receive his incredible peace, a peace that fills our souls with immense love. Filled with Christ, we experience awe, humility, and appreciation for being loved. Filled with Christ, we can do nothing less than exude and share that love. That must be the core of stewardship.

How can we describe the sense of joy there is abiding within Christ? Forgiveness must be easy because our only desire is to keep the Holy Spirit present in us.

So convicted, I receive a glimmer of understanding about how the human Jesus attracted disciples. His God-light emanated so brilliantly that the pure of heart could only be drawn to his immense love. Jesus could not sustain so bright a light without giving it to others. Love is a powerful force that spreads outward in joyful song.

God is the song present in the mystical instrument that is our soul. Open in his love, saying yes to stewardship as gift makes perfect sense.

I know that I will cross icy roads again and that my anxiousness will return, but today I am grateful for the fullness of God's love. A fullness that stands alone. It no longer matters how I am clothed or adorned, what I eat, or what burdens that I carry. Only walking in God matters.

And so I pray: I bow my head with tears of joy on my face and words of praise in my heart. In you, I am complete.

47 *Grace*

At some point in our lives, each of us reaches the crossroad where we must choose one direction over another.

Throughout my life, I have had the honor of spending time with people and hearing their stories, inspiring stories about real people standing at the crossroad and heading into the wind. Emotional stories filled with the elements of struggle, sorrow, trust, and God's redeeming grace.

What captures me most is how people conquer the struggles in their lives. A husband and wife choose to have a baby they learn will be born with a chronic disease. A woman loses her job to illness but finds spiritual resurrection in redirecting her energies to church. A young man goes to prison for drug trafficking and comes home to change the course of his life. A workaholic experiences a crisis that jolts him back to family.

The stories are not told dramatically, but in quiet voices filled with humility and a sense of awe at how God lifts us with his grace.

Even more so, the stories fill me with an awareness of how closely our walks parallel that of the Holy Family's. Mary chose to bear Jesus. As the handmaiden of the Lord, she was filled with God's grace. Joseph chose to accept Mary. He is honored as the Son of Man's earthly father. Jesus chose the cross—he suffered, died and was buried, and on the third day he rose again. Fully trusting in God, they walked in his direction to glory. God gifted them to us as role models.

Many of the sorrows we face are not the result of wrong choices on our walks, but of living in an imperfect and sinful world. As we grow in faith, we realize the difference between the crossroads we choose out of integrity, and the self-imposed burdens we carry resulting from our own poor choices. Although we try to deceive ourselves, we cannot liken the latter burdens to Jesus falling while carrying the cross. It is when we accept to walk God's path that our cross is lightened by his love and grace.

Grace comes out of sorrow and struggle. Grace leads us to joy. We do not expect to be exalted as Mary or to achieve sainthood as Joseph. In our daily walk with God, we simply have a need to share our stories of sorrow and struggle, and love and trust with each other. To evangelize Christ. To bring others to the eucharistic table. We are disciples.

48 *Consumerism*

The average home size in the United States has more than doubled since 1950; many Americans don't pay their bills on time or balance their checkbooks; and financial problems seem to be one of the primary causes of divorce.

We live in a consumer society, our economy based on debt. Excluding mortgages, our debt load from credit cards, student loans, and loans for cars and other purchases reached nearly $2.8 trillion in December 2012. Taking on debt to buy a bigger house or car or to secure a better position is only one symptom in the disease of affluence that subtly erodes our spiritual lives.

The need to possess is also a symptom that is just as tragic. For example, this week I met with a delightful young woman in her mid-twenties. She and her husband have been married for two years. They are cradle Catholics who married in the church, her husband graduating from Catholic schools. Both are hard workers, and have good jobs.

They bought a $100,000 home that they are paying off within ten years and are saving for retirement. They drive modest cars, have no debt, and are very responsible. They are a good hard-working Catholic couple.

When I asked her about their goals, her response was that they want to be debt-free by thirty so "we can travel and buy lots of toys." Although they were raised and married in the church, they have not registered at a parish or in any way become involved in ministry. They are winners in the quest for the American dream.

A dream that—as my husband so eloquently states—is like chasing bubbles. We race to catch a bubble. When we catch it and it pops, we are disappointed to find there is nothing solid inside. To feel happy again, we have to chase and catch another bubble. And so, we continue to accumulate toys as our joy continues to dissipate.

Gregg Easterbrook talks about America's affluence in his book *The Progress Paradox: How Life Gets Better While People Feel Worse*: "Most of what people really want in life—love, friendship, respect, family . . . does not pass through the market." He reports that in 1957, 3 percent of Americans felt lonely, and now 13 percent do.[1]

A *Newsweek* review of Easterbrook's book hits the nail on the head, concluding, "Affluence's afflictions endure and remind us of an eternal truth: it matters, as individuals and as a society, not just how much wealth we have but how well we use it."[2]

If we want the joy of living fully in the Holy Spirit, we have to renounce the emptiness of consumerism and take up the walk as disciples of Jesus Christ. Practically, we must choose to use the riches God has entrusted to us for *his* intended purpose. Until we make the decision to realign our prayer lives, personal goals, and household budgets to adhere to God's blueprint, we are compromising the depth of our relationship with *him* and the spiritual power we receive to serve him.

We cannot say, "I give of my time, therefore I should not be expected to tithe." We cannot say, "I will volunteer after my children are grown." As stewards, we relinquish control of treasure, time, and talent just as we have relinquished our will to God. Simply put, we respond to God's call by giving our all.

We can no longer justify our lack of giving by demanding control over where our money is spent, expecting recognition for our gifts of time, or attaching strings to sharing our talents. They are not ours to control. We have to transcend from an attitude of "what do I have to give up?" to an attitude of "what else can I give?" "What other need may I help fill?" "What am I doing to bring others to Christ's true church?"

Stewardship is not about what the church expects or needs; stewardship is about our need to respond with all that we are and have in gratitude to God. If we want our children to embrace discipleship, we must take the risk first: the risk to trust God.

The risk to make the conversion to stewardship in our own hearts, in our daily walk, in our prayer life, in holy adoration, in our Mass attendance and participation, in receiving the Eucharist, in building our family budgets, in our service to others. We need to give all in order to create an atmosphere of stewardship in our homes and parishes.

As the bishops' Pastoral Letter on Stewardship states, "This conversion of mind and heart will not happen overnight, but, as always, the Holy Spirit is at work in the Church today. Those parishes and dioceses that embrace the theology and practice of stewardship are beginning to see a change of attitude on the part of clergy, religious, and lay people" (51).

It is an attitude surrounded by joy.

Notes

1. Gregg Easterbrook, *The Progress Paradox: How Life Gets Better While People Feel Worse* (New York: Random House, 2004), 177.

2. Robert J. Samuelson, "The Afflictions of Affluence," *Newsweek* (March 21, 2004).

49 *Following Christ*

Belief in Christ is not found in debate but in wholly giving ourselves to another in love.

That is the sentiment I want to express to a loved one who nurtures his cynicism for God and church. His e-mails and phone calls depict nonbelievers (himself) as rational and intelligent and believers as gullible and weak (me). Fast-talking and awaiting the next comment, he pounces on my words, never hearing but wanting only to sway me to the empty side of life without God.

I am inadequate in rebuttals, not interested in the exhaustive process. Faith is not something I can or care to argue. Overpowered by his verbal blasts, I accept that my choice to follow Christ sets us on a divisive path.

Life's path has many setbacks and the cynic views Christians as those who need a crutch to get through it. With no vision, therefore no hope, of the eternal they cannot fathom as rational that Christian aspirations are not bound by a short time on earth, but by the desire of life forever with God.

A cultural lie promoted as norm is that love of self means reaping for oneself. When Jesus spoke about loving our neighbor as ourselves, his words were to inspire us to give all of ourselves from the depths of love. Continually giving/emptying ourselves of love, we are, paradoxically, replenished with greater and more abundant love. Faced with cynics, we must wonder why they have lost the courage to love. What closed their hearts in fear of giving themselves totally to others?

Think of our family members, spouses, children, and friends— those we consider important to us. If we are too controlled, too proud, too afraid to open ourselves fully to them, how will we ever experience the fullness of love Christ wants to give us? One who does not give all, give freely, and give until emptied does not receive all either. Therein is the loss of cynics. Misguidedly defining strength as invulnerability, intellectualism as the foundation for existence, they have closed their hearts to receive love. Not believing in God, they live in a faded world, never seeing the richness and depth of its true color.

Humans do not exist on an intellectual sphere alone; rather, we are imbued with souls—the spiritual and moral force—to complement our brains. A life of fact and analysis devoid of soul is narrow and shallow, and it erodes us. One focused on self-satisfaction denies the responsibility implied in love of neighbor that is the crux of Jesus' message.

Living for our own satisfaction is like standing alone in an unstable building on shifting sands. Without a moral foundation, our "needs" become whims that are forever changing and never achieved. Dissatisfied, we turn to find no one left beside us.

The challenge to the cynic is this: keep an open mind and repeat the mantra, "If there is a God, come into my heart."

Have the courage to find and accept the love awaiting you.

50 *Temporal vs. Eternal*

"If there are no obstacles, what do we need to do to be stewards?" Bishop Bernard Harrington of the Diocese of Winona, Minnesota, challenged us in his address.

On the seven-hour road trip home from the conference in Omaha, I had plenty of time to reflect on his words. I remember praying, "Show me the way, Lord. Let me do your will." At that precise moment, I realized my limitations as a steward come from only focusing on and desiring the temporal versus the eternal; the times when I want what I have never had or—to be honest—needed. For, you see, focusing on the temporal is typically an "it's all about me" activity.

Temporality is a restless state of being, whereby we jump ahead to the next want, event, or activity to keep us in the center of, as my now adult nephew Zach said in his younger years, "where the action is." It is a childish longing for more that is never quenched.

The eternal, on the other hand, leads us to quiet where we find our soul's rest in God alone. It is in prayer that we discover our role as disciples is simply to be God's messengers. To bring others to him through the love we share. The same love that God has for his son Jesus.

Jesus prayed submersing himself in the quiet of the desert, mountainside, and garden. Thus refreshed and invigorated by communion with his father, he returned to the real "action," teaching us the message of eternal life.

"Reflection, contemplation, and prayer are not something to pass the time until the Church can get back to work—they are the work of the Church," Fr. Raymond de Souza commented in response to how the church would function in the interim between Pope John Paul II's death and the election of his successor.[1]

Prayer is the state of being from which our true longing for the eternal emanates. Prayer is what leads us to discipleship, to live as joyful, grateful, and generous stewards. "Love others and pass along my message of joy," is all God asks. Steeped in his love, our desire for the temporal fades to a whisper.

We teach the message in many ways, not all of us through words. Like the apostles we act it out by visiting the sick and imprisoned, feeding and clothing the hungry, comforting the lost, and even rejoicing with other Christians. Putting on this face of Christ, we are natural evangelizers. The fruits of the Holy Spirit—among them kindness, joy, goodness, and love—are magnets that attract others to our Christ and thereby God.

Winding my way home, God again shows me that abandoning my soul to love is the only way to live a life of discipleship, a life of stewardship. Temporal desires are the obstacles I must shed as the weight that slows my travels to him.

As I pull into the driveway and shut the car door, it occurs to me what a balancing act this life on earth is. A scale seems an inadequate image to depict living in Christ. Rather, it is the constant interplay of faith, prayer, and response to God that molds us into willing disciples.

And so I pray: Dear Lord, let me love without holding back.

Note

1. Raymond J. de Souza, Holy Post, *National Post* (April 2005).

51 *Serving God*

On a Saturday in 2005 I sat in the east terminal of St. Louis Airport, watching the National Guard fighter planes take off, wondering if they were heading for the disaster of Iraq or New Orleans. Having put Mom on a plane to return home to Tampa, I waited to ensure it took off without a hitch.

As always, ours has been a lovely visit, and our good-byes touch us both with a hope to be reunited again soon. It gets harder to have Mom leave, feeling that it's time for her to be close by. These past two weeks devoted to her have filled me with an unexpected grace.

No matter how full my life, I find there is always room for more caring. Despite the tumult of scheduling and putting my responsibilities on the back burner, this time set aside just to address Mom's needs and hopes for the future fills me with a sense of responding as I should.

That response leads me closer to God's center. In relationship with Mom, I find strength in Christ and a strengthened relationship with his Father, my Father, my God.

Imagine the flow of love in our lives if we can give up our needs, knowing God will take them lightly on himself. For our burdens, regardless of their weight on us, are but feathers in the hand of God.

Sometimes, the dimension of our love flows out of how we pray.

"Let it be for you" is a standard beginning for many of my prayers. Going to Communion Sunday morning, I proceeded through the line in just such a fashion praying, "Let this moment, this day, this week, this lifetime be only for you, Lord." Immediately I realized the nuance in my prayer that would make it deeper: "*I offer* this moment, this day, this week, this lifetime to you, O Lord."

We do not need God's permission or action to receive him. We need only to offer ourselves to him. I became conscious of how passive "Let it be" sounds. How, unthinkingly, we call the Lord to be the initiator in our lives. We speak of being "called to serve," a state that has us waiting on a notice from God instead of calling God ourselves.

Calling on God doesn't translate into our acting hastily without thought or marching ahead as if leading a crusade. Rather, I think of calling on God as a definitive statement, as ready acknowledgment of his unwavering presence. It seems to me that God waits on us much more than we ever wait on him.

The idea that God waits on us is probably simpleminded in many ways. I can only conceive of the concept as a parent gauging the depth of her children's spiritual development and, regardless of its growth, waiting for a deeper enrichment in their discipleship. How God waits on me, I do not know. I only know—just as with my mother's—I do not doubt God's love and care.

And so I pray: That the families of Iraq, New Orleans, and all who suffer from war and disaster do not doubt God's love for them, but claim the strength of his infinite presence to care for each other.

52 *Waiting for Conversion*

I found it on an extemporaneous shopping trip to Springfield—the chest of drawers that fit the look I've envisioned for our bedroom. Exquisitely hand painted in lush reds and greens, it will complement the floral painting my husband lovingly gave me and my great aunt's chair we had reupholstered in a knobby green and yellow pattern.

A woman of many wants, finding the chest sent redecorating and color schemes swirling through my thoughts. A new living room carpet and an antique walnut chair were next. The credit card company is pleased.

Were I to examine my motives, creating pleasing spaces proves a good reason for my purchases, as does the pleasure of reward earned from long and hard work. Yet, a third, and most revealing, motive is the desire to rearrange uncertainty in my life through solid wood and fabrics—things that I can touch and see and organize to suit me.

After all, they are much easier to arrange than circumstances or feelings expressed with insufficient words. In a moment of humble lucidity, I asked the Lord to distinguish between my needs and my wants and to supply my needs beyond my wildest expectations. Afterwards, I promptly shelved the prayer among my daily schedule.

God heard me. Within days I received a call from someone whom I have not heard from in many years. Pacing as I struggle to unravel the story of seventeen years, I am unable to put into words its sequence or sentiments, finally realizing that to everything there is a season and this is not yet the season for the story's unveiling. There is more truth and grace to uncover.

Through signs and whispers in the wind, God divulges truth to us, which we acknowledge by the absence of any doubt. There is no wavering in God's truth, no shades, and no uneasiness. For those are gone, long worked out along the path toward acceptance of his way. With that truth, we can readily accept those who have stumbled along the path fully aware that we, too, are sinners. We have stumbled.

And we learn a truth: that without the guidance and giving of God's pure love, we cannot find his way. We cannot hold on to people, pleasure, or property, hoarding them in the fear of our loss. It is in giving away in love that we shine. Not in buying and arranging furniture. For there are no sentinels guarding God's gate. His door is always open in the great hope of receiving us all.

In this glimmer of God's powerful truth—that we minutely comprehend and accept—is love.

And so I pray: Bring the seasons as you may, Lord. For you alone truly know our needs and inordinate strength to follow your path.

53 *Inspire Me*

I walk the dusty road and listen for the whisper of the Lord. I hear the expectant call of a bird waiting for its mate to reply, and scan the branches of the walnut trees until I spot a diminutive indigo bunting, its robust call so disparate with its small size.

I listen to the water trickling down the rocky slope of the hillside into the creek and wait for its music to embrace me in comfort. Today, to no avail.

It is hot and the deer flies and gnats circle and buzz around me annoyingly. The gravel is hard on my feet and the cars that go by without slowing fill my throat with dust.

These are the times when my spiritual well runs dry. My mind wanders listlessly, thinking neither light nor deep thoughts, but bouncing back and forth in a dull grayness. I feel as though I am trekking through the desert, shriveling with thirst and longing for replenishment. "Inspire me, O Lord" is the only prayer that makes it to my lips.

Why do we have these dry times? What must we do to return to the Lord? How can we shake the sand off our feet?

We live in a world packaged with *instant*: instant oatmeal, hot water, news, and gratification. The thought of one thousand years being the blink of an eye to God exasperates us. The world is our oyster and we want to partake of everything—*now*. But that isn't God's way. "All in due time," is his message, "I am beside you in the desert."

Whether we come to the desert from doubt, the death of a loved one, or desires gone unfulfilled matters little. Our biggest challenge is to trust that God remains with us. Trusting in his omnipresence, we can accept our time in the shadow and use it to listen, observe, and, most of all, pray.

Many long years ago, Ignatius wrote to his sheep, guiding them with the reminder that "man is created to praise, reverence and serve God our Lord, and by this means to save his soul. The other things on the face of the earth are created for man to help him in attaining the end for which he is created."[1]

God gave us his loving son to keep us on the road to home. Our ultimate home, where we meet Christ, is at the altar. It is by partaking of the Eucharist—the body and blood of Christ—that we are recreated, rejuvenated, and refocused to praise, reverence, and serve God. The dry times are when we especially need church and community.

And so I pray: Hear our cry for inspiration, dear Lord. Bring us to our knees and fill our minds, ears, throats, and hearts with your abundant love. Bring us to your light.

Note

1. Saint Ignatius of Loyola, *The Spiritual Exercises of St. Ignatius*, ed. Louis J. Puhl, SJ (Chicago: Loyola University Press, 1952), 12.

54 *Asparagus*

There is nothing as good as freshly steamed or sautéed asparagus. Regrettably, its growing season is short and the bed that bears such a sweet tasting repast looks overgrown and mangy most of the year. One of the first summers we were married, I surprised David by weeding the asparagus bed. I pulled and tugged in the dirt until I'd cleaned it all out, satisfied when the raised area looked as tidy as his well-tilled garden.

Little did I know, the scruffy looking stalks I yanked up produced the energy essential for its roots to grow next year's healthy crop! Needless to say, we didn't eat homegrown asparagus the following spring.

At times my thoughts seem to mirror that asparagus bed. I get confused between what spiritual strengths to nurture and what weaknesses to weed out. Ask me to name my strengths and weaknesses and I can easily jot a few down under each heading. But, I find that without God, all the strengths I list are false. I cannot write them down without remembering every time I have failed. I lose heart and slide down the pit of self-doubt.

Yet, God, my parent, knows my heart and what I need to cultivate healthy roots rather than weeds. Solomon acknowledges this, saying, "You spare all things, for they are yours, O Lord, you who love the living. For your immortal spirit is in all things. Therefore you correct little by little those who trespass, and you remind and warn them of the things through which they sin, so that they may be freed from wickedness and put their trust in you, O Lord" (Wis 11:26–12:2).

Long dead for centuries, St. Ignatius continues to teach us the merits of examination of conscience, prescribing a linear method of prayer to expel our human weaknesses.

But I find myself turning to St. Teresa of Avila's *Interior Castle* for the comfort of her wisdom. She speaks to me more than the men of old; her words directed to women—her sisters in the convent—in ways that I identify with. In simple yet elegant terms she shares, "If we turn from self towards God, our understanding and our will become nobler and readier to embrace all that is good: if we never rise above the slough of our own miseries we do ourselves a great disservice."[1]

She is quick to convey the importance of self-knowledge, tying it all the while to the danger of breeding self-doubt that paralyzes our spiritual growth. Not to chide us or belittle us as can be true of scholars of the rule, but to open our souls to God's glory. I am grateful for her elliptical thinking, which gently nudges me to step out of my asparagus bed.

"For although, as I say, it is through the abundant mercy of God that the soul studies to know itself, yet we can have too much of a good thing, as the saying goes, and believe me, we shall reach much greater heights of virtue by thinking upon the virtue of God than if we stay in our own little plot of ground and tie ourselves down to it completely."[2]

So, I am encouraged to venture out of my well-tilled self-indulgence, reflecting instead on taking God's chosen path for me. It is not mine to understand or fret about the way God uses me, only mine to keep opening the door to my soul wider and wider so God may shine through me. I will proceed with faith, believing in St. Teresa's assurance that when I pull the stalks instead of the weeds and fail, "do not lose heart, or cease striving to make progress, for even out of your fall God will bring good."[3]

And so I pray: Help me hear your Word, dear Lord, and live in your guidance. Take my will. Let it vanish in the wind. Keep what is good to reseed your garden and let the wind scatter the rest.

Notes

1. Saint Teresa of Avila, *Interior Castle*, ed. and trans. E. Allison Peers (Mineola, NY: Dover Publications, 2007), 38.

2. Ibid.

3. Ibid., 51.

55 *Highway Thoughts*

In the last six weeks, while logging five thousand miles on my odometer, my head has been filled with disjointed thoughts and random musings.

Being present. Celebrating Mass as a visitor at Holy Family Church in Columbus, Georgia, I realize how blessed that I am. The phrase "be present" continues to sing or float through my thoughts. Be present to others, each moment there to serve. Sometimes the serving (in God's name always) is simply to listen, other times to act. Always to welcome and invite, for being present is the crux of being Christ and community. And so I sing: Let me be present, be present, be present. Let me be present, O Lord. In all that I do, with all whom I meet, let me be present, O Lord.

Offering myself to God. Going to Communion, I wonder if by simply not looking and listening we keep God at a distance. Proceeding through the line in just such a fashion, I am overcome with the realization that we do not need God's permission or action to receive him. We need only offer ourselves to him.

Listening and learning. Attentive to each other, we can plant conversion seeds, a point of view, a position, and let those around us discuss and debate. Taking in other viewpoints to quench our thirst, we learn beyond our narrow selves. Most important, an easy quiet from the outset allows others to speak their mind without defensiveness, only to express for learning's sake. What a joy to loosen my opinion, letting it carry itself into the atmosphere, where it will fly or burst without bruising my ego or that of those with me; rather, we can enjoy the exchange at no risk and much potential reward in creating beyond our own limitations and imaginations.

Servitude. What amazes me is that our servitude takes many forms, varied by individual approach. For example, this week we shared our home with visiting family. Yesterday morning, I awoke and made my usual toast and coffee for breakfast. Opening the yogurt spread I put on my toast, I noticed that whoever enjoyed it before me had taken the knife to the bottom of the tub and scooped out a slice of the spread from top to bottom.

I have never thought of taking spread any other way than filling my knife by skimming it across the top of the spread, leaving the surface even. But, I quickly observed that "cutting" into the spread yielded the strawberry deposited in the middle. In my preference for keeping a smooth (could it be calm?) look, I have been forfeiting the taste of fruit in each bite!

Joy. "Joy is an incredible inner sense of being blessed and filled with goodness," said the priest at St. James Parish in Kearney, Nebraska, this Mother's Day. It reminds me of a needlepoint picture my sister made for me that hangs on my kitchen wall: "Take joy from each day." I want to rewrite it to say, "Give joy in each day."

56 *Acts of Kindness*

I heard a news story a few days ago about a waitress receiving a $10,000 tip from a customer. She paid for her meal with a charge card, wrote in the tip on the appropriate line, added up the total, and signed her name to officiate the transaction.

At first, the waitress and restaurant manager thought it was a joke. But it wasn't a joke. It was a gift. Perhaps it was a pure and simple gift made in a moment of impulse. Or perhaps the giver had carefully thought out her action ahead of time, taking pleasure in finding that one person who smiled at her just so, or seemed needy, or poured her a cup of coffee with care. Who knows what rationale warranted such a gift!

We are left with the affirmation that a small act of kindness on the part of the waitress reaped an extraordinary act of kindness in return. The acts of giving and receiving have a symbiotic relationship, the achievement of each resulting in mutual joy. Being on the receiving and giving sides of kindness changes our lives.

Lately, my husband has spurred me back into bike riding. He has a hybrid bike built to ride on the road or trail. I haven't owned a bike since someone stole the one my parents gave to my sister Kathy and me for Christmas back in the 1960s. Come to think of it, I never actually rode that bike, seeing as it was stolen that same day. However, that's beside the point.

The point is we've been riding on the trail all season with our good friends Judy and Larry. We meet them at Dotty's Café in Hartsburg most Saturday mornings, and, for the first couple of weeks anyway, I rode a bike we rented from the Hartsburg Cycle Depot. Kind folk that they are, Larry and Judy decided to lend me one of their bikes to get started on. Kindness to them is a daily part of their lives, and I'm sure they haven't given their act of sharing much thought since or made me feel beholden to them. Judy and Larry are just naturally generous.

However, their simple act of kindness has released a deep sense of gratitude in me. While riding down the trail, I am grateful for the surrounding nature, the bench we frequent that Ken and Pam Hall donated for trail users to rest on (another kind couple), having joints that work, and even the soreness that sets into them after our ride. I am grateful for their friendship and the mutual respect and acceptance it furthers.

Surely, acts of kindness are seeds planted by the Holy Spirit to awaken us to the goodness inherent in one another. To bring us to those "Aha!" moments whereby we *experience* the meaning of Jesus' great commandment to "love one another as I have loved you" (see John 13:34). He unifies us to become his disciples, giving to and receiving from one another.

I'd like to think that the spirit of kindness has settled naturally into my bones, undistinguished between friends or strangers, those I get along with and those whom I have a harder time liking, much less loving. God continues to teach me that the more kindness I give and receive, the closer I am to experiencing unconditional love. The more I love my sisters and brothers that, as Jesus said, "I can see," the greater is my understanding and acceptance of God's love for me and mine for him.

I don't suppose a $10,000 tip will fall into my lap anytime soon, but the simple act of lending me a bike fills me with a richness that will only increase as it is shared.

57 *Blessings and Talents*

Across the street from our church is a wall surrounding a schoolyard on which the children have painted a colorful mural. Inked on the wall is the mural's title, "Blessings and Talents." I think how appropriately it blends into our eucharistic prayer for God's healing and the love with which he blesses us. For his blessing is just the beginning of our Christian lives. We are called to take God's gift of love and share it with others.

God is love expressed through friendship, discipleship, sacrifice, and using the talents with which we are blessed. This truth is claimed in Psalm 47:8: "God is king over all the earth; / sing hymns of praise" (NABRE).

Stewardship is the expression of our talents by, for, and through God. We are witnesses to God's love through the gifts he gives us, through the use of our talents—today. Today is the only day that counts for God. We face each day in the awareness that we are living it for God. In the parable of the talents, Matthew reminds us that it is the good and faithful steward who grows God's talents that receives great responsibilities and shares in his master's joy (Matt 25:14-23).

Everything we have comes from God. We own nothing but only manage the gifts he gives us. We are challenged to build our inner strength and confidence in the knowledge and faith that God wants us to share in his joy.

I can only believe that it is our duty to secure the spiritual, educational, and material needs of our family and community. Surely God is not suggesting we ignore our needs and those of others using the well-worn adage that he will take care of us. After all, he even quit providing manna from heaven to the Israelites he sent to wander in the desert! Rather, I believe that God is telling us to plan through him.

God is our filter and all that we plan and secure should be done through our love for him. Each day we plan, each issue we face, each challenge we address must be through prayerful consideration of God's will—truly, through the voice of God. We must look beyond ourselves toward God, consoled in the warmth of his love and prepared for the work he brings us.

For it is through his grace and forgiveness that we thrive, through acceptance that we come to terms with our growth. Without judgment or condemnation we see God in each other and appreciate the gifts we bring to his table. We betray our identity in God through doubt, rebellion, and pride, becoming gods or masters ourselves. Following in Christ's footsteps demands that we relinquish the control culture and riches have over us. "No one can serve two masters," he succinctly told the apostles (Matt 6:24).

God calls us to be frail and vulnerable, mortal except in him. He allows us to let go of control and domination of plans, time, and others. Doing so gives us patience in his way, relishing the path he has in store for us.

And so I pray: May we stay centered on your love and Word, dear Lord, in all that we do.

58 *Healing of Possessiveness*

We have a major shortcoming, a fault that I suppose is not unique but, rather, one most of us struggle with: we want to be fulfilled. After all, we are surrounded with the message that we are unique children of the universe who can accomplish anything we want, that we deserve to have everything we desire. These words and images swirl around us everywhere, in movies, magazines, newspapers, self-help books, television, and billboards. Even our educational systems tie our children's futures to building financial and social success.

We spend our lives filling our homes with things, our stomachs with food, our minds with trivia, and our time with pleasure. To maintain this lifestyle, we continually empty our garbage, gas tanks, and bank accounts. We never stay filled.

At what point, then, do we empty ourselves to be filled by the gift of the Holy Spirit? It is very difficult to hear God's call when we seek fulfillment in the realm of the transient.

Stewardship calls us to clear our psyches of the advertising messages implanted there since birth to encourage us to buy and spend. They are false messages meant to provoke within us feelings of fear and insecurity that without possessions we are powerless and our lives hold no meaning.

"We need stewardship," says Bishop Felipe J. Estévez of the Diocese of St. Augustine, Florida, "to heal possessiveness." For it is possessiveness that Americans suffer from most. Bishop Estévez's message is rich with the understanding that it is in relationship that we are fulfilled. First, in our relationship with Jesus Christ; then with our families, brothers and sisters in faith, and community.

Stewardship calls us to recognize that eternal value lies only in Christ's great commandment to love one another. Stewardship challenges us to release ourselves, to stand naked, offering up to God our wills, hearts, and plans as gifts.

And so I pray: Dear Lord, heal me from the need to possess. Give me eyes to see my brother and sister beside me, a heart to love them, and a mind focused on building your kingdom.

59 *One Thousand Crowns*

Thy name, thy kingdom, thy will. At first it was the alliteration that caught my ear. But it was hearing the speaker talk about the phrase's profound truth that kept my attention.

> Our Father, who art in heaven,
> hallowed be thy name;
> thy kingdom come,
> thy will be done
> on earth as it is in heaven.

Thy name, thy kingdom, thy will. These simple words encompass the totality of our calling as disciples. We praise God who comes first, we look for the coming of eternal life that is heaven, and we commit ourselves to do his will. Paul explained it thus to the Corinthians: "Think of us in this way," he says, referring to the apostles, "as servants of Christ and stewards of God's mysteries" (1 Cor 4:1).

It rained tonight, perhaps heavily enough to uproot and wash away the fourteen inches of topsoil that covers the one thousand crowns of asparagus we planted on Saturday.

We had calculated the space we'd need and decided on a location with good access and runoff. Our neighbor brought over his tractor and plowed the field for us, churning up the rich soil that lay under what we have always taken for granted as mere "lawn" that is pretty to gaze upon when mowed. Then David tilled and retilled the field, loosening the thick clumps of dirt into powder.

Saturday's effort began with David tilling long rows with a distance of two feet apart and digging eight-inch trenches by hand. Laura and I followed with the crowns. They look like octopuses: a head that bears the asparagus with roots dangling below like arms. One by one, we took a crown, fanned its roots out in the dirt so that its head faced skyward in their center. We eyeballed the recommended distance of a foot or so between roots and repeated the action one thousand times.

After planting, we took the hoes and stood at opposite sides of a row, taking turns covering the crowns with the dirt David had unearthed, first one side and then the other until the whole field boasted long lines of dirt mounds. And then, with sore backs and a feeling of accomplishment, we rested.

A neophyte to farming, I am awed and humbled by the natural relationship that exists between working the land and God. To understanding in part Paul's description of being "stewards of God's mysteries."

Farming opens your heart to beauty and mystery and service. Its entire purpose is to share. We work the field in an orderly way, following the process step-by-step to cultivate a good and enduring crop. The joy is in the work and the anticipation of bringing healthy food to the table.

Two springs will pass before we begin to reap the harvest. Last night's storm found us hoping that the one thousand crowns will have at least a year to take root without the creek rising to flood stage. It rarely does so, but we have no control of the weather. We plant and watch as our work unfolds.

Thy name, thy kingdom, thy will. We praise his name, his gift of the soil, and bend our will to cultivate disciples.

And so I pray: Dear Lord, thank you for opening my eyes and heart and hands to the beauty of life. To you, I offer these one thousand crowns.

60 *Respect*

Western philosophers have discussed the concept of "respect for persons" since Immanuel Kant placed it "at the very center of moral theory."[1] Kant believed in the innate dignity of all, and that respect should extend to our elders, those in authority, the weak, the powerless, and even criminals. Respect outweighs our desire for reward or return; rather, it is focused on treating others with value. As St. Augustine pointed out, "If you never turn aside from the good life, your tongue may be silent, but your actions will cry aloud, and God will perceive your intentions; for as our ears hear each other's voices, so do God's ears hear our thoughts."[2]

For Christians, having respect falls naturally within our framework of serving God. "As servants of God, live as free people, yet do not use your freedom as a pretext for evil. Honor everyone. Love the family of believers. Fear God. Honor the emperor" (1 Pet 2:16-17). Peter's words speak to us in this Easter season, reminding us of Christ's dignity in suffering.

The worthy wife in Proverbs 31:10-31 is a fitting example of a woman who lived as a servant of God. Verse 18 serendipitously entwines our desires with hers: "She enjoys the profit from her dealings" (NABRE). The passage intimates that she enjoys her work in and of itself. She may very well enjoy both, but the point substantiated by the entire dialogue is that she is not anxious about tomorrow, but instead that her peace and joy stem from ensuring that the needs of others are met.

Faith—she has a strong religious spirit; she "fears the Lord." The Bible explains this is "reverential awe and respect toward God combined with obedience to God's will" (NABRE n. to 1:7). In her reverence and respect for God, the worthy woman places her trust in God, relinquishes her will to him, and practices goodness and justice toward others.

Family—she cares for her husband, children, and household. The first point of the story (v. 11) is that she is in a loving relationship. Her husband entrusts his heart to her and she, in turn, "brings him profit [good], not loss [evil], / all the days of her life" (v. 12, NABRE). Theirs is a marriage of trust and commitment.

The worthy woman recognizes that from the beginning God created us for family and she maintains a tight-knit relationship with her husband and children for life. The members gain their strength and joy from each other.

She is also a good manager, a steward who deals with producing and buying and selling goods, working with merchants, and using her profits for sound investments.

Community—as befits a good steward, she tends to the poor and needy. Her care does not end with her family. Blessed with a love that cannot be contained, she naturally extends her hands and arms outward toward all.

The gifts she receives include trust, strength, dignity, joy, kindness, wisdom, and praise. She is the ideal wife or woman because she has excelled in proven worth and is sanctified by her efforts. Internally, her success is joy and laughter. Externally, her works praise her at the city gates.

She exemplifies Paul's treatise on disciples: "For this momentary light affliction is producing for us an eternal weight of glory beyond all comparison, as we look not to what is seen but to what is unseen; for what is seen is transitory, but what is unseen is eternal" (2 Cor 4:17-18, NABRE; see 4:16–5:10).

And so I pray: Dear Lord, let me meditate on *respect* and *dignity*, fusing them into this way of life that is yours.

Notes

1. Robin S. Dillon, "Respect," *The Stanford Encyclopedia of Philosophy*, Fall 2010 Edition, ed. Edward N. Zalta, http://plato.stanford.edu /archives/fall2010/entries/respect/.

2. Saint Augustine of Hippo, Sermon, *Liturgy of the Hours*, vol. II (New York: Catholic Book Publishing, 1976), 865.

61　*Spirit*

We loaded our bikes onto the back of the truck late Saturday afternoon and drove to the parking lot in Hartsburg beside the entrance to the Katy trail. No sooner had we found that sweet rhythm of pedaling that begins alleviating the stresses of the day, than we were warned by approaching bicyclists that the trail ahead was closed. Hesitant to lose our momentum, we kept on. As soon as we crested the levee, we came to a halt, unable to cross the chocolate-colored mud covering the once-smooth flat surface. Though the wrong color, the view looked like a scene from Seuss's *Bartholomew and the Oobleck*.

On Monday evening David and I tried a different tack, parking the truck north on a side road above the levee. The lower fields on our left along the river stood in water, but, with its higher elevation, for two or so miles the trail was untouched by last week's flooding. What a joy it was to ride the familiar path under a canopy of trees as shelter from the wind!

Our joy was short-lived, as further up its path of drying cracked mud looked like icing on a cake that had been slathered with chocolate chunks. Since it was unsteady riding, we dismounted our bikes and pushed them through the ruts.

On this breathtaking clearing sits a humble home on stilts. It faces the river to its west, and its back to the bluffs on the east. We only know of the older gentleman and his dog living there, used to seeing him outdoors mowing the extensive lawn, puttering in the flower beds, or sitting under the shade of the patio. This evening, gone was any hint of greenery, a hue of dirt offering the only color for miles. True to his nature, we found the old man tilling the earth in preparation to reseed the yard.

Regardless of the flood damage to his "property"—which thankfully was comparatively minimal this time around—the man labors for the soil, the river, and the bluff that are God's.

"When you . . . [t]ake away their breath, they perish / and return to the dust. / Send forth your spirit, they are created, / and you renew the face of the earth," the psalmist says (Ps 104:29-30, NABRE).

These are words that may be taken for granted by those who love and work the land. For they endure the fruitless years of drought, disease, or flooding with the hope that comes from experiencing abundance. They have faith that what nature takes away, God will renew.

We say our hellos and express our concerns and encouragement to the smiling old man as he works. Uplifted by the Spirit, we remount our bikes and ride on.

And so I pray: For those who love and care for this earth and sky, Lord, that you fill their hearts with the fullness of your Holy Spirit.

62 *Wind*

For the first leg of our twenty-mile trip we rode our bikes effortlessly. With the wind at our backs, we switched into high gear and maintained faster-than-usual speeds. At the halfway point, we dismounted and sat by the river to sip our drinks. We chatted, then fell into contented silence, feeling a certain reverence in watching the yellow finches fly by, the sun reflecting through the clouds, and the stillness of the water.

The wind picked up, dipping low to create waves that sent fallen trees, plastic bottles, and flotsam hurtling down the river in an offensive, trashy looking display. Dragged underwater by force, the buoy marking the channel repeatedly plunged and then reappeared on the surface like a porpoise diving through the air.

With our sense of enjoyment disrupted, we remounted our bikes, pointing them windward toward home. Pedaling was not so easy on this second leg. Shifting into lower gear, we tightened our grip on the handlebars to steady the bikes and pumped our legs harder against the wind's force. We felt the road's dust settle in our throats and stick to the sweat on our arms and necks. Riding was hard work. Every so often, one of us glanced down at our odometer, and shouted to the other, "7.5 more miles to go," "4.8 more miles," etc. It was a long, tiring ride that left our leg and shoulder muscles aching.

At home, asparagus waited to be picked and family members to be taken to a concert. We create the work that is never done, and relish the play that is never enough!

When enjoying what we do, the wind seems a breeze that floats about gently cooling and refreshing us. But, when life becomes tedious or overwhelming, when we lose sight of its purpose, our efforts are like fighting a blinding wind that leaves us dry and stripped down. Unlike the buoy marking the river's depth, we plunge and dive without an anchor to steady us. We ache for relief. *Relief*, however, comes only through *belief*, in accepting that the wind will always change direction.

Instead of fighting the wind, we take on the challenge to "Fight the good fight of the faith" (1 Tim 6:12). We reorient ourselves to view the wind as analogous to the breath of the Holy Spirit: of receiving the Holy Spirit each time we inhale, and unleashing the Holy Spirit each time we exhale. With every breath we inhale, we invite Christ in and accept his gifts of "righteousness, godliness, faith, love, endurance, gentleness" of which Paul speaks (6:11). With every breath we exhale, we give witness to Christ and invite others to come to him.

Fighting the good fight is work that is rewarded by God, "who richly provides us with everything for our enjoyment" (6:17). In God, the winds of work and enjoyment complement one another.

And so I pray: Let me not despair when the wind is at my face; rather, strengthen my faith to give and receive your Holy Spirit.

63 *Mother's Day*

We all love hearing the story of how our parents met, picturing them in their youth and imagining their lives before us—the kids.

My mother and father met at a New Year's Eve dance in Mexico, Missouri. As the story goes, Dad's date got sick at the dance, introducing him to Mom on her way out. Evidently, they clicked. Dad left early to attend Midnight Mass at St. Brendan's Church, gallantly inviting Mom to go with him. Having been raised a "nondenominational Christian," as Mom says, she wasn't too keen on the idea of stepping into a Catholic church!

Dad's faith was uppermost in his life. After all, he had served as a Christian Brother for nine years, in part, teaching at Boys Town in Omaha under its founder, Fr. Flanagan.

Mom managed the savings and loan company in town, the first of two women to be promoted to that position nationally. "And," she still likes to emphasize some fifty years later, "I was paid the *same* salary as the men."

Born in the small town of New Bloomfield, within the "Kingdom of Callaway County," Mom admits to being well-loved and maybe even pampered a bit as a child. Her dad had struggled with tuberculosis for several years, ultimately dying in an asylum in Texas when Mom was eleven or twelve. My grandmother Lucille supported Mom and her younger brother Jack, working as a secretary at the Missouri School for the Deaf in Fulton.

Mom and Jack spent lots of time at the New Bloomfield News, helping their grandfather publish the town's paper. And, with no children of their own, Aunt Gladys and Uncle Scott were second parents to Mom. As a matter of fact, Mom's mannerisms and love of shopping can be directly attributed to Aunt Gladys!

Dad must have really wowed Mom, because she converted to Catholicism for him. They married two days after Christmas in the Immaculate Conception Church in Jefferson City. Uncle Scott and AG, as we called her, held their reception in their home on Ewing Street. A framed picture hangs on our stairwell of Mom in her ice-blue wedding gown surrounded by her bridesmaids.

Mom and Dad had a great life together, with laughter, tragedy, and adventure stirred in. They moved to Michigan, where they had seven kids in eight and a half years. A favorite story of theirs goes something like this. Mom's family warned her that a future married to a Catholic meant she would always be expecting a child and would be stuck at home. After producing two boys and then a girl, one family member remarked with finality, "Now you've got your family." From then on whenever they were expecting, rather than telling the family, Mom and Dad let them know by sending out a birth announcement!

Polio was the frightening disease at that time. One morning little Jimmy Pat seemed to be sleeping in late. Mom went to check on him and found him to be "not quite with it." She called Dad at work and he met her at the hospital, but too late. Only two years old, Jimmy Pat died within a few days—polio of the brain was the diagnosis. I didn't understand losing a child until I myself had children. As a youngster, I remember thinking, "at least they had other children to take care of." I imagine the grieving never really goes away.

With the last baby just three months old, Mom and Dad packed up the six of us and moved to South America. Actually, Mom did the packing. Dad had gone ahead to DC to prepare for his new position with the US Agency for International Development. Imagine packing up a house and traveling alone with six little ones! What a great sense of adventure my Mom has.

Mom was finally vindicated from her family's prediction that she'd be "stuck at home." She had a great time inviting them to visit her overseas.

There is a deep well of love, caring, and emotion that doesn't really shine through words on a page—especially about our parents.

This Sunday will be one of the first in my adult life to celebrate Mother's Day with my Mom living nearby. I hope she knows the depth of my love and caring for her.

64 *Boxes*

Family members tease me about being compulsive, watching me straighten the house before going to sleep and repeating the same task before I leave for work each morning. I confess that I like returning to a home without clutter, with the beds made and the kitchen counters cleaned. Admittedly, my tendency to pick crumbs off the floor could be considered on the edge of compulsive behavior.

Therefore, it jarred me when—living my life in the orderly box that I like—the world stepped inside and threatened to shake it up. As with my neat house, I became territorial. What values are in the box that I protect and carry around with me like a security blanket?

Accomplishment is one, crossing items off a to-do list giving me great satisfaction. Certainly, believing in my ability is another. Expressing my opinion is a strong third-place contender. Having any of these values challenged shakes me into acting territorial. And, that is not a pretty sight.

Therein lies the log in my eye. For God little cares how I perceive myself or assume others perceive me. In God's eyes, my value lies only as a beloved child, placed here to fulfill his purpose. Once I accept that fact, my desire to control the environment around me is no more effective than the apostles wanting to sit on Jesus' left and right sides. Jesus came as a servant and died because his perfection threatened those tied to the values of the world.

In our human frailty, we do not have the spiritual strength to protect ourselves from the world. The world "offers temptation to lead us astray; it strikes terror into us to break our spirit," St. Augustine wrote. "At both of these approaches Christ rushes to our aid, and the Christian is not conquered."[1]

Often we create obstacles hindering God's position as number one in our lives. When the sirens of success and greed tempt us. When we forget to pray. When we develop sloppy and undisciplined habits. When we succumb to the values of pride, power, and pettiness.

To cleanse us from straying God allows us to be tempered by fire. "Where is your security now?" he might ask, reminding us to refocus. Turning our faces to him, we thank God for staying steadfast despite our lowly ways, singing the praise of Proverbs 18:10: "The name of the LORD is a strong tower; / the just run to it and are safe" (NABRE).

Our safety lies in invoking the name of the Lord in prayer. God's tower releases us from the need to be territorial and allows us to achieve our purpose on earth. God's tower protects us from the world's changing winds, keeping us firmly tethered on his path. When we cast the logs out of our eyes and into the fire, they emit much more warmth and help us convert those in the world. Admitting our frailty helps us love the enemies who shake our boxes.

We follow where we feel secure. That is what is so jarring in following Christ. On the one hand, we know we are led to God, yet, on the other hand, it is frightening to give up control of how Christ will lead us to God. For we are nudged by Christ to take the hard and narrow path without planning, rather, to let Christ move us where he will. Christ has us risk everything in his name, secure in the belief that the unseen road leads straight to God's home.

Note

1. Saint Augustine of Hippo, Sermon, *Liturgy of the Hours*, vol. III (New York: Catholic Book Publishing, 1976), 1316.

65 *Wonder*

Whether circumstantial or divine, it seems fitting that the results on voting for the new seven wonders of the world have just been released, for dancing through my mind has been a bit of G. K. Chesterton's alliteration from *Orthodoxy*: "We need so to view the world as to combine an idea of wonder and an idea of welcome."[1]

As a child I sat with my family in the small train as it ascended 2,300 feet up the Corcovado Mountain in Rio to stand beneath the 100-foot tall statue, Christ the Redeemer of the Open Arms. Mounted on a 20-foot pedestal overlooking the Atlantic Ocean, Sugarloaf Mountain, and Copacabana beach, Christ the Redeemer welcomes visitors to Brazil. I have no recollection of the train ride, but succinctly remember (in wonder) that Christ's little finger was larger than I!

Wonder feeds our soul and heightens our sense of awe so that it is natural for us to proclaim, "Bless the LORD, my soul; / and do not forget all his gifts" (Ps 103:2, NABRE). I can't say if Chesterton ever saw the Christ the Redeemer statue, but he understood that wonder opens the soul to unbounded beauty, art, and poetry. And, where beauty, art, and poetry reside, there also is welcome.

I walked outside this morning only to be welcomed by the dawn air scented with jasmine and dew. Drops of that dew were captured in a filigree-patterned spider web woven overnight to span the width of our water garden. My spirit soared with joy from creation's humble offerings as it went about its purpose: jasmine enticing bees to make honey; dew quenching the earth and its insects' thirst like manna; the spider building its trap, unbeknownst it is an artist.

Without knowledge or sense of purpose, the jasmine, the dew, and the web feed nature's creatures. Only the human soul is cognizant of nature's design. Only the human soul can view and express the antics of creation as beauty, art, and poetry. Only we can glory in the wonder of God, the creator.

Thus blessed, we too are moved to create. Whether simple or staggering, minute or magnificent, our work is meant to inspire, to share, to make us leap with the joy of accomplishment, to open our arms like Christ the Redeemer welcoming all not just to Brazil, but to the City of God.

And so I pray: Dear God our creator, we praise you for blessing us with the gifts of wonder and welcome. Help us keep our souls open to receive them.

Note

1. Chesterton, G. K., *Orthodoxy* (New York: Doubleday, 1959), 11.

66 *Twine*

There was a crazy kind of game that I remember my parents staging at a dinner party they hosted several years ago. Before the guests arrived, they took balls of twine—one per invitee—and went throughout the living room stringing twine high and low, around and under the furniture, until each ball had been unraveled and they had created an intricate cobweb.

Each guest was given the end of a twine ball with instructions to follow its path, rewinding it as they went along. There was a lot of laughter as the guests reached over doorways, crawled under chairs, or wove around each other to rewind their balls of twine! Reaching the end, they received their reward—a ticket redeemable for dinner. It seems to me the twine game is analogous to our Catholic faith. Both take us to high and low points, around obstacles, and both require negotiating relationships. We have the choice of approaching our faith from an attitude of joy or all wound up in knots. Lately, I wonder if we haven't chosen the latter.

We spend a lot of time worrying about "competing" with nondenominational, Protestant churches that have magnificent shows and seem to have mastered uniting evangelization and entertainment. We view ourselves as the big ship that can't turn around quickly enough to be in the race for members. But is unraveling our course truly our goal?

Instead, let's adopt the strategy to *focus on what we do best.* Instead of fretting about what the "competition" is doing, let's offer our "product" based on *its value.* Let's get excited about the strengths we hold, such as

- family,
- Catholic education,
- liturgy,
- sacraments, and
- social justice.

We are the universal church that focuses on the needs of the soul, responding to questions such as these:

1. What do I hunger for? We hunger for love, acceptance, and community. As church, *we focus on* welcoming others into our lives, our homes, our activities, and our circles.

2. Where do I go to be fed? We believe that family is the first nutrient and, as church, *we focus on* serving the family.

3. How am I fed? Just as we have an innate desire to be one with God, so that desire leads us to the Word, and the Word leads us to serving others. While God is always present to us, we realize that presence the more we serve. As church, *we focus on* sharing Christ's presence in the

Eucharist, teaching the Catechism, and leading people to serving others.

4. How do I feed others? We follow Christ's command to Peter to "feed my sheep" by our acts of charity and service. Most important, *we focus on* accepting that everyone has gifts to offer and nurturing the use of their gifts rather than dependence. People experience love, acceptance, and community where their worth is recognized.

Waiting for us at the end of our ball of twine is the earthly reward of dining at the eucharistic table and anticipating eternal life with God. We have the choice of meeting God with joy or wound up in knots. Let's focus on the former!

And so I pray: Dear God, we praise you for the gift of choice. Help us focus our perspective on the gifts we have rather than those we lack so that we may plot a course based on our strengths.

67 *Hot Summer Days*

How can it be August already? I have yet to swim in the pond or go out for ice cream or take long, carefree weekends lounging in the sun. Yet, tax-free back-to-school shopping days have come and gone and we find ourselves ensuring Laura has all her required immunizations before she goes off to college in seventeen short days.

While summer is going fast, I am amazed at how quickly thirty-one years of parenting have flown by. Thirty-one years! I am savoring the moments Laura squeezes in for us between making her final rounds with friends and family.

Last Saturday the three of us stayed home and froze sweet corn. This year, David was ferocious in guarding his beloved crop from deer and other critters. Just as it tasseled, he put up an electric fence around the corn and gridlocked an acre perimeter of the field as well. Barring major shocks, nothing, man, mouse, or muskrat, was going to get in David's corn. His vigilance worked, as no critter did, including Laura or me. David picked alone.

Over the years, we have honed our vegetable processing down to a science. Our goal is to keep as much dirt and mess out of the house as possible. So, we found the inch of shade the patio offered and shucked the corn outside, cleaning off the silk and throwing the stalks into plastic bags. David set a pot of water on top of the propane heater to boil, stuffed as many ears as would fit into the aluminum basket, and immersed the basket into the water until the ears were parboiled or blanched.

Lifting out the basket, he let the water drain out of the holes in its bottom and deftly dumped the golden yellow corn into a large cooler fed with cold water from a garden hose. Once Laura and I finished shucking all the ears, we headed inside to the (air conditioned!) kitchen to complete the final step: we cut the blanched and cooled niblets off the cob and scooped them into quart bags. Every now and then we'd stop to pick a few cuttings out of the bowl and eat them.

When it was all said and done, thirty-six-and-a-half quarts went into the freezer downstairs. To be truthful, setting them in the freezer wasn't the last step, cleaning sticky corn juice off the floor and chairs was.

Call it teamwork or many hands making light work—whatever expression you favor—as a parent I know that the shucking corn, canning tomatoes, playing rummy, hanging out times are the ones I will miss most. It's around the kitchen table that we get to know our kids.

Jesus understood the power of communion, the ever-binding yet precious power that compels us to openly spread our hearts and dreams out on the table for all to partake of and embrace as one.

Last night, Jake called and asked me how I made cooked carrots in brown sugar. You never know what part of their past our kids take into their future.

And so I pray: Dear Lord, keep us ever mindful that hearts unfold and blessings are created through simple activities shared.

68 *Freedom*

Last night I had a curious dream. David and I were at Mass with our daughter Laura. Nothing unusual about that except that in the dream she was a toddler instead of an adult. Rather than crossing her arms to receive a blessing from the priest during Communion, the two-year-old Laura extended her hands to receive Communion. Naturally, the priest (unidentifiable in my dream) and I quietly corrected her. Back in the pew, I looked around and she was gone.

I raced out of the church and down the basement steps into the adjoining school hallway looking for Laura. Some older kids said they had seen her but didn't notice the direction she was headed. My last thought before waking was one of concern: "I hope she isn't outside on her own."

All week long friends have asked me how it feels to have our last child out of the nest. "She's been gone less than a week!" I've replied, silently proud of myself for managing so well. However, I must admit that in addition to last night's back-in-time dream, every now and then I've caught myself listening for Laura's familiar movements in the house.

Dropping her off at college last weekend marks the first of many things for all of us. It is the first time in our twenty-year marriage that David and I have been without children. It is the first time Laura has had to share a room with someone—high time in our consideration! It's the first time we need only consider what we want at the grocery store, or what we want to do, and so on. We are as giddy by the freedom we have earned as she must be on her own in college.

While sitting on the bench in front of the student union last Saturday, I absorbed the energy swirling around the campus with the return of the kids. It brought back memories of my freshman year of college and the English teacher who encouraged me to keep writing. I thought of all that Laura will learn about the world and her purpose in it. I thought of her talents and raw skills that will be honed and polished until they shine and bring glory to God.

These thoughts bring me full circle to the Catholic schools in our own diocese and the children who grow to their fullness through the academic, spiritual, and social education they receive here. We are blessed to have the advantage of tuition-free schools, parishioners who support them, teachers who live out their vocations, and parents who eagerly involve themselves in their day-to-day functioning.

I suppose each generation grumbles about the challenges of financing education—from kindergarten through college—and we are no exception to feeling the pinch. "Now that we have the freedom we can't afford to go out" is a phrase we can take to heart! But what a joy it is to see the wonder in our children's eyes as they grow in understanding and take those steps toward independence. Watching my children makes me realize how little I have sacrificed yet how much I have received.

And so I pray: Dear Lord, I thank you for every step of our journey as parents, the sorrow and joy, the giving and receiving, and the memories and times yet to come.

69 *Economics of Food*

I looked down at my dinner plate and realized that everything we were eating came from our farm: crappy and catfish we caught in our pond, and eggplant, zucchini, cabbage, onions, and tomatoes we grew in our garden.

We are so incredibly blessed to be able to connect what we eat to its original source. As participants, we understand the labor and care it takes to produce food—the weeding, the sweat, the disgust at the rabbits that eat the green beans before they can climb the trellis to safety, and the well-fed deer and raccoons that will polish off the sweet corn as soon as it tassels unless you set out the dog to chase them. Since creation, the fact that the earth produces food to sustain us continues to be a miracle.

With the prevalence of prepackaged, frozen, and chemically engineered "food" that is purchased at competitive prices in a Wally warehouse, it is difficult to imagine—much less experience—food as miracle. For most, the only toil connecting us to what we eat is our once-a-week trip to the store where we push a grocery cart with a wayward wheel down an overcrowded aisle and feel frustrated standing in the line staffed by the slowest checkout person, ever.

Since the industrial age, "economies of scale" has proliferated as the marketplace mantra. Big is cheaper and more efficient. Automation requires less labor and therefore more profit. Globalization allows goods to be shipped and consumed anywhere. While goods may be cheaper, we pay the cost by losing the intrinsic value of producing our basic needs.

Our nation's bishops take up this call, noting, "Every perspective on economic life that is human, moral, and Christian must be shaped by three questions: What does the economy do *for* people? What does it do *to* people? And *how* do people participate in it?" (USCCB, Economic Justice for All 1).

Keeping the discussion on our food source, one can argue that with globalization we have access to a greater array of food than ever before. We can get oranges year-round instead of as a treat in our Christmas stocking, as was true in years gone by.

By the same token, our stores' shelves are a glutton's delight, where the selection (and probably purchase) of junk food far outweighs that of fresh produce. And, even with all this food at our fingertips, we still don't produce home-cooked meals most evenings or sit around the Lord's table as family or community to eat. Rather, two to three times per week (at a minimum), we load up on the unhealthy alternative of fast food on our way to games, practices, work, or meetings. Doing so, we lose the sacred ritual of preparing, offering, and sharing a meal that nourishes both body and soul.

As adults, we pay this price ruefully, yearning for simplicity, for time to slow down, for demands to lessen. What is startling for us to consider, though, is that most of our children don't know there is a different way. Having grown up in a fast-paced, plentiful world of consumerism, will they understand the principles of economic justice? Can they take to heart that they have little or no control of producing the food they eat? Will it disturb them to know that five firms hold 42 percent of our nation's retail food sales, four firms process half of all broiler chickens, and 80 percent of the soybean market is controlled by four firms (USCCB, For I Was Hungry and You Gave Me Food)?

The flaw in a profit-based economy, says author Joseph Pearce, is "the failure to recognize humanity's ultimate dependence on the natural world" and "whether goods are man-made or God-given, whether they are renewable or otherwise."[1] His points speak to the stewardship of creation: God created the world, and entrusts it to us for its care and cultivation. As partners with God in this "divine human collaboration," we are called to make *life* flourish (USCCB, Stewardship: A Disciple's Response). The economy can only be deemed good insofar as we flourish in God.

And so I pray: Dear Lord, you gave us the beauty of the earth as a gift. Open our hearts in recognition, our backs in labor, our hands in sharing its riches with one another, and our souls in praise to you.

Note

1. Joseph Pearce, *Small Is Still Beautiful: Economics as if Families Mattered* (Wilmington, DE: ISI Books, 2006), 18.

70 *Salsa Days*

This season the garden reaped little corn. There was no summer day when we called family to help pick the ears, shuck the corn, clean off the silk, parboil the ears, and, with sharp knives and warnings of caution, cut the succulent kernels off the cob for freezing. There was no banter, mess on the kitchen floor, or dividing the goods among family to store for winter consumption.

While we lament the corn dried on the stalks, our loss is lessened by the abundance of juicy tomatoes on the vine and our subsequent salsa-making days! For three weekends now we meet on the farm to can. We pick the tomatoes and jalapenos, and dice onions and tomatoes by the gallon. The younger children clamor to help, so we set them up peeling the garlic cloves. In assembly-line fashion, we wash and fill pint and quart jars, carefully cleaning off the rims before putting on the boiled lids and rings. Lifting the hot jars out of the pressure canner, we gather around the table in vigil waiting for the sound of the *pop* that guarantees a good seal.

We divide the salsa among the households. "Store the jars quickly before the neighbors see them," we tease. Like the little red hen hoarding her homemade bread, we are still too tired by our labors to consider generosity. Admittedly, we know the satisfaction of seeing our work lined up on pantry shelves is fleeting; eating our goods at an empty table offers no long-held joy.

In recent years many in our nation have experienced economic downturns. Regionally, we hear those having the hardest times are farmers, small business owners who rely on contracts from larger agencies not currently outsourcing, employees of factories that are closing, and the retired whose investments are on a slow rebound. Some are leaving their communities to seek jobs elsewhere. Times are tough all around, so it seems.

The tough times test our generosity. The widow with her mite and Solomon with his riches symbolize a generosity born of gratitude, caring, sacrifice, joy, and faith that goodness will be rewarded.

Gratitude is thankfulness for life. Gratitude is the knowledge at the core of our hearts that we are children of God, his DNA woven as gift in our mothers' wombs. As the prophet says, "For I know well the plans I have in mind for you—oracle of the LORD—plans for your welfare and not for woe, so as to give you a future of hope. When you call me, and come and pray to me, I will listen to you. When you look for me, you will find me. Yes, when you seek me with all your heart" (Jer 29:11, NABRE). Wow.

Caring is an outgrowth of gratitude. Caring comes easily in our lives when we grow beyond ourselves, realizing that we are connected one to another. We are the family of man depicted in the coffee-table book of the same name.

There is truth in the statement that those lacking the spirit of generosity do not acquire it when they obtain riches. Whether talking about financially supporting our churches, reaching out to those in need, or sharing our talents, each one of us is called to sacrifice from our staples, from the milk we drink, not just the cream. What sacrifice do we make when we give out of our excess? when we give our spare dollar, or spare coat, or spare time?

If we consider others as members of our family, we give them our most precious gift—our hearts. Generosity stemming from our hearts is suffused with joy. It is a reflex response born of our inherent need to give, not from the need of others to receive (as attested in the USCCB document Stewardship: A Disciple's Response).

Generosity is not a foolish faith that irresponsibly claims God will take care of us with no effort on our part, but the core belief that our lives will be enriched by following Jesus' path. Faith is letting go of our will to ultimately inherit a glorious eternal life. "Let us not grow tired of doing good, for in due time we shall reap our harvest, if we do not give up" (Gal 6:9, NABRE).

This winter, when we gather around the table once again, we will talk of snows yet to fall, and enjoy the vegetable soup made with a rich tomato base from this year's crop. It matters little that corn is missing from the soup, for now we have chips and salsa on the side! Next winter we may have corn and no tomatoes. Who cares, whatever we got we'll share.

And so I pray: Dear God, if there is a gift I have given my children, let it be the spirit of generosity born out of gratitude.

71 *Special Graces*

Our parish started Happy Feet, a dance group that meets one evening a month. Influenced by *Dancing with the Stars*, David and I took to the floor, as I visualized us—over the course of time—waltzing together all lightness and grace. Oh, but time has since been otherwise filled and we have yet to practice the steps we learned or go for lesson number two.

Will I ever be graceful on my feet?

In today's breviary reading, St. Cyril of Jerusalem refers to Corinthians, in which he hears the melodies of grace in the various gifts of wisdom, teaching, preaching, and prophecy. "A special grace," St. Cyril calls this faith given to us by the Holy Spirit.

> Now this kind of faith, given by the Spirit as a special favor, is not confined to doctrinal matters, for it produces effects beyond any human capability. If a man who has the faith says to this mountain *move from here to there*, it will move. For when anybody says this in faith, believing it will happen and having no doubt in his heart, he then receives that grace.[1]

Will I ever have the grace to move mountains?

It is within Mary, full of grace, that our Christ first resided as man. All accounts of Mary portray a woman who responded to life with grace, a loving mother who filled her heart with the love of her son—as we mothers do, though ours are not the Perfect One.

Will I ever have the grace to love?

I fall short of all comparisons, all examples of grace. Not a dancer, earth mover, or blessed mother am I, but simply a woman struggling each day to live in God's Word, emulating faith until I accept the special graces residing within me and let them flow naturally from my heart.

Through St. Paul's teachings we know that faith, hope, and love mark us as Christians. Taking this journey on earth, we are called to walk in faith, filled with the Holy Spirit. We are called to radiate love with a strength that sparks hope within those we meet. And where there is hope, there is joy.

Hope and the joy it engenders are special graces natural to me. They are the gifts God has designed within me for his purpose.

And so I pray: Continue to hone me so that all my hopes of dancing, moving mountains, and loving be yours.

Note

1. Saint Cyril of Jerusalem, Sermon, *Liturgy of the Hours*, vol. IV (New York: Catholic Book Publishing, 1976), 485.

72 *Talent*

The first poem I remember writing was when I was recovering from rheumatic fever as a child. Though it's long been lost, the recollection of the poem left behind with me is one of fairies dancing around a fire. In school, I loved writing papers and knew I was good at it, but it wasn't until college that I began to recognize writing as a *talent* I held. And that only happened because of my English teacher. She assigned the class to write a paper describing what we saw out of the classroom window. To my absolute astonishment, she read mine out loud to the class before handing it back to me. She had written the following note in the upper right-hand corner of the paper in pencil: "Come and see me when you are ready to take off on your own."

One of my biggest regrets in life is that I never took her up on the offer. You see, at nineteen, I wasn't confident enough to understand the opportunity she was offering me, mature enough in my faith to realize that talent is a gift from God. Nor did I fathom that this gift freely given to me would multiply in value through its use for God.

Through a series of positions, my career has progressed in such a fashion that I now claim writing and communication to be core to my purpose in life. So much so, that when I write or speak about living a stewardship way of life, a central focus is on discovering, defining, and delivering our talents and helping others do the same.

I share this bit of my search with you because I believe you have traveled or are traveling the same path as I: desiring to fulfill your purpose in Christ. With that, I offer the following Scriptures and resources to ponder and pray over as you continue on the quest to discover your gifts and to nurture them in others.

Discover

"Now there are varieties of gifts, but the same Spirit; and there are varieties of services, but the same Lord; and there are varieties of activities, but it is the same God who activates all of them in everyone" (1 Cor 12:4-6).

Define

"Iron sharpens iron, / and one person sharpens the wits of another" (Prov 27:17).

"So with yourselves; since you are eager for spiritual gifts, strive to excel in them for building up the church" (1 Cor 14:12).

Deliver

"What shall I return to the LORD / for all his bounty to me?" (Ps 116:12).

"So let us not grow weary in doing what is right, for we will reap at harvest time, if we do not give up" (Gal 6:9).

"I can do all things through him who strengthens me" (Phil 4:13).

"Above all, maintain constant love for one another, for love covers a multitude of sins. Be hospitable to one another without complaining. Like good stewards of the manifold grace of God, serve one another with whatever gift each of you has received" (1 Pet 4:8-10).

And so I pray: Dear Lord, as we reflect on your son, Jesus, freely giving his life that we might have eternal glory, grant us the clarity to discover the gifts you have placed in us, the focus to define those gifts, and the joy in delivering them for your purpose.

73 *Home*

In ninth grade our class read *To Kill a Mockingbird.* Though it was the first high school I attended out of three, I still remember my English teacher. She was old (probably no more so than I am now), had glasses, and wore her black hair pulled up in a teased bun that sat atop her head. Barring offense, she looked like a made-to-order cartoon caricature.

"She was probably ready to move anyway," I responded when the teacher called on me to answer her question about how Scout's aunt must have felt when her house burned down. Startled by my reply, I can still see her face and hear her words back to me: "Jane, I'm surprised at you; you're usually more intuitive than that." I guess she expected me to say something like, "Well, Scout's aunt is making the best of a terrible situation by acting like the house meant nothing to her, but inside she is filled with grief and sadness."

Having moved every two years of my life, grieving for a house was anathema to me. Houses weren't home or security. Home and security were family, and I carried them with me wherever we moved.

The two are no longer mutually exclusive, my home being the open door that my family bounces in and out of. As the parent, "home" to our children means the farm, their old bedrooms, and the attic where their childhood memorabilia is stored. I'm not sure what they would say if David and I were to ask them if the farm meant security to them. While the three know they are being bequeathed equal shares of the farm, none of them consider making it their homes when David and I bite the dust.

When I asked Corey if he'd ever want to live on the farm, his reply was "I can't live in a house I haven't built myself." Jake and Sarah have plans to travel the world and Laura's immediate goal is to leave the nest, not inherit it!

No, the kids do not see the farm in their future plans; rather, it is their past security and, because it's home to me and David, their current link to that security.

Last night's newspaper carried a picture of an Iowa neighborhood that was devastated by a tornado. That's what got me thinking about the meaning of home. As a Christian steward who believes everything I have belongs to God, I have to question if God is so central in my life that my possessions have little hold over me. Could I come up from the root cellar after a tornado, thank God for sparing me, and praise him for the blessings of family, security, and love?

I don't know if the answer I gave in ninth grade would be the same.

And so I pray: Dear Lord, may those whose lives are uprooted by nature's whimsy know that home is in the Eucharist.

74 Upside-Down Truth

I don't have an entertaining story to share with you this week about canning salsa, riding bikes, or the always hysterical (to me, anyway) antics of my children. Rather, my time has been allocated in small chunks to a myriad of projects, events, and discussions, leaving me no opportunity to unravel any thoughts that may be lingering about in a tangle. Please pardon my impudence for asking for your help in working through my primary conundrum of the week: Is shaded truth still truth?

In a recent discussion, a friend of mine and I agreed that the values of the world are upside down. Political campaigns, breaking news, consumerism, international conflicts, the state of the economy, and so on are large-scale examples where telling the flat-out truth has gone by the wayside. Truth, it seems, is being shaded or erased to sell one's governing capabilities over another's, to tell a good story, to obtain luxuries, to deny a nation's responsibility for starting wars, and to argue whether or not the economy is tanking.

It is fairly easy for most of us to shrug our shoulders in hopelessness when it comes to suggesting solutions to re-right our nation, much less the world scene, on *telling the whole truth, and nothing but the truth, so help me God*, as courts require of witnesses. At its simplest, the question begs, Do I as an individual always tell the truth?

The cynic may respond that telling the truth—or abstaining from lying—is not one of God's commandments. He or she may argue that the eighth commandment, "Do not bear false witness against your neighbor," specifically and only applies to publicly accusing others of something they did not do. The humanist may take the cynic's stand even further, denying the existence of God in his or her refutation.

For those of us who believe in God and God's commandments, any time we lie we bear false witness. Whether we tell little white lies to spare someone's feelings or whoppers to avoid conflict or deflect our stand on an issue, try as we might to justify our reasons, lying is lying.

On a personal level, we can't get by with shrugging our shoulders in hopelessness for lies we have told or truths we have shaded. For we are gifted with a conscience that knows truth, and a soul wherein the Holy Spirit lives and nourishes us with God's pure love. It is up to us to acknowledge our own sinfulness, seek forgiveness, and focus on our journey to holiness.

And so I pray: Dear Lord, help us to deny the values of the world that woo us with twisted words and messages. Lead us through prayer, to hear and spread your truth.

75 *Debt and Faith*

I admit it. I forwarded an e-mail I received from Dave Ramsey. For those of you unfamiliar with him, Ramsey promotes debt-free living through his book *Total Money Makeover*, in his *Financial Peace* seminars, and on his radio and television programs. The e-mail I forwarded had to do with Ramsey's solution for the economic crisis in 2008—a counter to the $700 billion government bailout.

What I want to address is a reply I received from a friend and colleague who responded that Ramsey's solution is not in line with Catholic teaching. "Taking care of one's self," my friend wrote, "is part of the Protestant work ethic . . . the notion that God rewards those who help themselves." Catholics, rather, are distinguished by their "sense of working for the common good" and that "God rewards those who put the needs of others first."

His two cents rendered me speechless and feeling somewhat tarnished in the faith department. It seemed that having a work ethic devalues one's Catholic foundation and trying to do well for oneself means one is less sympathetic to or generous in addressing the needs of others. I didn't realize the two were mutually exclusive.

On further reflection, it came to me that, regardless of their faith, people thrive with the presence of two elements: purpose and hope.

God creates us for and with a purpose and embedded within that purpose are the following stewardship principles: recognizing, using, growing, and giving back in abundance from all that God has blessed us with. To discover and maximize our purpose, we must actively pursue it. And that takes discipline and work. Being disciplined and working—firmly grounded in purpose—does not guarantee an inflow of money nor a desire to accumulate stuff, but it does lend itself to greater happiness. Even our Declaration of Independence claims man's right, not to happiness, but to the "*pursuit* of happiness." Conversely, regardless of our wealth, if we find no purpose, if our lives are aimless and random, we are unhappy, lonely, and without hope.

Hope is found first and foremost in our love relationship with God, knowing we are bound together for eternity. Second, hope leads us to aspire for something better, such as a better job, health, circumstances, understanding, or relationship. Hope does not exist in a vacuum, but springs out of our incompleteness and need to be in full relationship with God and our neighbor.

Christ didn't say love thy neighbor *not* thyself. Rather, he counseled us to love our neighbor *as* ourselves. Having discovered our purpose is in and of God, that he has placed within us this gift of life to be used for him, we come to realize that we are loved ones of God, intricately bound one to another in him.

On a surface level, I do understand my friend's chicken-and-egg hairsplitting between the two faiths. Some Protestant denominations do teach that God will monetarily reward those who give their lives to him. Our Catholic stand is less about the amount of coins one has and more about thankfully using and returning the coins we do have to and for God's purpose.

Regardless of this difference, and I suspect others, we are brothers, sisters, neighbors, and children of the same wonderful God and that fills me with hope.

76 *Shrines*

Set in a terra-cotta shrine, the household goddess rests on a rectangular pedestal. With hands folded in her lap and long hair flowing over her chest, she has sat there since crafted during the Iron Age in 800 BC, serenely taking in all that occurs outside her temple arch.

The plaque I read at the Museum of Art and Archaeology potentially identifies her as Astarte, the fertility goddess worshiped by the Phoenicians of the Mediterranean coast. Descendents of the Semitic Canaanites, the Phoenicians were adventurers who built boats from cedar trees. They sailed the sea far from their home in modern-day Lebanon to England and Africa, even establishing a colony in Carthage.

They traveled the Tigris and Euphrates Rivers, carrying lumber, glass, copper, and bronze to other cultures and leaving behind the alphabet we use today. Kings wore the purple linens the Phoenicians dyed from the ink of shellfish.

How amazing it is to consider that whatever we procure, we have always needed to worship. In ancient civilizations, gods were in nature. The sea; sun, moon, and stars; trees and forests all were alive with wills of their own. In these mythical times before scientific knowledge revealed nature under the law of universal rule, and philosophy revealed we control our will, morality, and choice, all good and bad were attributed to the gods.

And so shrines were made to goddesses such as Astarte, kept in places of honor in homes and worshiped. "Bring us good crops; keep the rivers from flooding them; make us strong against our enemies; protect our homes. We bring you offerings; do not punish us. Our happiness depends on your pleasure."

We have much to learn from history.

In today's civilizations the idols have changed from those alive in nature to inanimate ones that bring us a sense of power, prestige, and momentary pleasure. Electronics; expensive cars, boats, airplanes; large homes for a family of three to four, and all the furniture we arrange in them. We know the list.

Ultimately, when nothing else satisfies, we seek God—inward for the gifts he has endowed us with, and outward to share them with our neighbors. We are disciples, dispelling the myths of old, and spreading the Good News of salvation in our travels, whether at home or on the internet or sailing across the world on the seas.

History reminds us that the longing of the soul continues beyond gold, copper, wars, plagues, flooding rivers, and civilizations lost and rediscovered. God the Creator—the *was and always shall be*—walks beside us today.

And so I pray: Dear Lord, you have given us souls to praise, wills to understand, and the choice whether to follow you. In our travels, let us leave behind your Word.

77 *Stompin' Feet and Wooing Souls*

This past weekend David and I enjoyed the season opener of the Columbia Civic Orchestra at the newly restored Missouri Center for the Arts. *Ragfare* featured the ragtime music of Scott Joplin as well as Beethoven's seventh symphony. One got our feet to stompin' and the other wooed our souls. Both linger long after we leave the theatre.

What made the concert inspirational is that, conducted by thirty-four-year-old Stefan Freund, the fifty-eight-piece orchestra is an all-volunteer one whose purpose is to develop and inspire local talent of all ages, spread the love of chamber music, and provide enjoyment for its members and audiences. Its spirit of sharing art, building friendships, and offering quality entertainment as a gift to the community is infectious.

With election hype spewing fear and futility we closed our eyes, ready to drift into the harmony with God and nature that good music creates. To open up to the spiritual realm that refreshes and reminds us of God's unchanging truth and love.

To soar with the promise that, regardless of present and future conditions, all is in his timeless hands.

As they concede loss and accept victory, our candidates speak unifying words. They agree to work across party lines, to keep America the home of the brave and the land of the free. Words to inspire, to abate the uncertainty of change and loss of position. But, as in all competitive races, there are losers and winners, the powerless and the powerful, seemingly trading places every four to eight years.

The Christian race has the highest stake: eternal life with God. While we look to the eternal, by the same token, we are called to immerse ourselves into the muddle inherent in our earthly communities. We are God's voice, hands, and feet. We are his disciples called to speak the truth above the din, cradle the forgotten, and walk beside the hopeless. This is a race in which individuals have the choice to win. God wants all his children to cross the finish line.

As disciples acting in stewardship, we look to Micah, a prophet of old, to find what God requires of us to carry his message of salvation to others:

> With what shall I come before the Lord,
>   and bow myself before God on high?
> Shall I come before him with burnt offerings,
>   with calves a year old?
> Will the Lord be pleased with thousands of rams,
>   with ten thousands of rivers of oil?
> Shall I give my firstborn for my transgression,
>   the fruit of my body for the sin of my soul?

> He has told you, O mortal, what is good;
> and what does the LORD require of you
> but to do justice, and to love kindness [mercy],
> and to walk humbly with your God? (Mic 6:6-8)

Justice, mercy, and humility. They are not precious items to be brought before the Lord like cattle, oil, or our firstborns, but values of the soul perfected in our daily walk with God. Our values shine forth as outward proof to others that here walks a man or woman of God. It is in the steadfastness of doing justice, loving mercy, and walking humbly that a steward attracts others to our all loving and eternal God.

We need only keep the melody of the words on our lips to get our feet to stompin' and get to wooing souls to God.

78 *Who Are We?*

Who are we? We speak of being disciples of Christ with stewardship as our way of life. First, we must *be in* Christ, and then it follows that all we *do* is for him. Of course, St. James clarified that faith and works are bound together:

> What good is it, my brothers and sisters, if you say you have faith but do not have works? Can faith save you? If a brother or sister is naked and lacks daily food, and one of you says to them, "Go in peace; keep warm and eat your fill," and yet you do not supply their bodily needs, what is the good of that? So faith by itself, if it has no works, is dead. (Jas 2:14-17)

This week we eat our bounty of turkey, mashed potatoes, sweet potatoes, green beans, homemade rolls, and pumpkin pie and express our gratitude for the table laden with food. We are indeed blessed to live in our nation's breadbasket, where gardens abound and fresh meat is plentiful. It is nothing for most of us to be well fed.

Ah, but do I feed my soul as much as my stomach? Does my demeanor reflect the growl of spiritual hunger or does it shine with the fullness of God? If I truly am in relationship with Christ, one in him, then where is the bounce in my step and my outstretched hands?

These are my simple thoughts after chatting with my sister Kathy this morning. As a flight attendant with Alaska Airlines, she lives in California, too far from home. She's single, and is working on Thanksgiving Day. It keeps her from missing family, pays double time, and, as she sincerely sympathizes, allows her married coworkers to spend time with their husbands and children.

We have often talked about how different our paths to God have been, yet how he has kept our hearts united. She laughs about our children's escapades, unable to relate to our parental reactions. I, in turn, listen to her stories of ministering to those who seek God as they are flying here to there in first-class seats. God's whimsical side was at work in giving Kathy a career as a sky disciple!

Let us give of ourselves in little ways, we agree, I knowing full well that Kathy is a save-the-world disciple who gives grandly. We end the conversation as we both head off to work, secure in Christ's love and guidance.

And so I pray: Dear Lord, as we prepare for this season's feasts, open your heart within ours so we may be your presence. Then we'll naturally give, our arms outstretched to others.

79 *Take My Thoughts*

Summer is winding down, vacations are memories, children are back in school, and committees once dormant are springing back to life, assigning their members tasks to meet their annual goals. We are a busy people, checking off accomplishments on the top of our to-do lists while adding more to the bottom.

At times we may find ourselves becoming frustrated with the complexity and fullness of our schedules. Some days we simply want to sit quietly, leaving the phone calls and e-mail unanswered. Some days our minds are so full of the cares of life that we cannot form prayer, though we earnestly desire to hear and follow God's call. Rather, we are like unattached kites, the wind pulling us one way and another.

Finding ourselves in times of spiritual flightiness, when we become stale and prayer seems reduced to utterances, there is a simple mantra we can recite: *Take my thoughts, dear Lord, and straighten their path in me.* For me, the mantra becomes a personal conversation with God, its meaning richly embedded with submission, reverence, appeal for guidance, and purity in action.

Take my thoughts: I humbly submit to you, Lord, who know my inner heart. I offer you my thoughts, asking you to claim me for your own. Take my will and mold it to yours.

Dear Lord: I sing praises to you. I come to you with reverence and the love of a child for a parent, awed by your perfect love for me.

Straighten their path: Left on their own my thoughts jump and turn from moment to moment, subject to subject. Unguarded, they are open to the wiliness of Satan's twist, to negative interpretations. As a result, my actions become reactive instead of prayerful responses to your guidance. So I ask you, God, to realign my thoughts, centering them on your will for me. Let me be a source of joy and healing.

In me: Move me to action. Help me open my heart to love others, to see you in the strong and weak. Help me see the face of Christ in others and act accordingly. Help me open my arms in tenderness and self-giving.

The late priest Fr. Henri Nouwen expressed these sentiments so clearly:

> The more willing I was to look honestly at what I was thinking and saying and doing now, the more easily I would come into touch with the movement of God's spirit in me, leading me to the future. God is a God of the present and reveals to those who are willing to listen carefully to the moment in which they live the steps they are to take toward the future.[1]

In simplicity, Fr. Nouwen reveals that to internalize God's spirit leads us to do God's will. There is a wonderful image of visualizing God as a circle and seeing ourselves inside that circle. We are in God, surrounded with and by and through God. We live each moment in God, not alone, but enjoined by our willingness to let go of ourselves and accept God's will. The words do not matter, only the openness of our hearts.

And so I pray: Take my thoughts, dear Lord, and straighten their path in me so I may reflect your joyful steward.

Note

1. Henri Nouwen, *In the Name of Jesus: Reflections on Christian Leadership* (New York: Crossroad, 1989), 154–55.

Selected Bibliography

Augustine of Hippo. *The City of God.* Translated by Marcus Dods. Peabody, MA: Hendrickson, 2009.

———. Sermons. *Liturgy of the Hours.* Vols. II, III. New York: Catholic Book Publishing, 1976.

Benedict XVI, Pope. Message of His Holiness Benedict XVI for Lent 2008. http://www.vatican.va/holy_father/benedict_xvi/messages /lent/documents/hf_ben-xvi_mes_20071030_lent-2008_en .html.

Catechism of the Catholic Church. 2nd ed. Vatican City: Libreria Editrice Vaticana, 1994.

Chesterton, G. K. *Orthodoxy.* New York: Doubleday, 1959.

Covey, Stephen, A. Roger Merrill, and Rebecca R. Merrill. *First Things First: To Live, to Love, to Learn, to Leave a Legacy.* New York: Simon & Schuster, 1994.

Cyril of Jerusalem. Sermon. *Liturgy of the Hours.* Vol. IV. New York: Catholic Book Publishing, 1976.

Doherty, Catherine de Hueck. *Poustinia: Encountering God in Silence, Solitude and Prayer.* Combermere, ON: Madonna House, 2000.

Easterbrook, Gregg. *The Progress Paradox: How Life Gets Better While People Feel Worse.* New York: Random House, 2004.

Hilary of Poitiers. *Liturgy of the Hours.* Vol. III. New York: Catholic Book Publishing, 1976.

Ignatius of Loyola. *The Spiritual Exercises of St. Ignatius.* Edited by Louis J. Puhl, SJ. Chicago: Loyola University Press, 1952.

Lawson, Douglas. *Give to Live: How Giving Can Change Your Life.* La Jolla, CA: ALTI Publishing, 1991.

Layard, Richard. *Happiness: Lessons from a New Science.* New York: Penguin, 2005.

Merton, Thomas. *No Man Is An Island.* New York: Barnes & Noble Books, 2003 (1955).

Muggeridge, Malcolm. *Something Beautiful for God: The Classic Account of Mother Teresa's Journey into Compassion.* New York: HarperOne, 1986.

Nouwen, Henri. *In the Name of Jesus: Reflections on Christian Leadership.* New York: Crossroad, 1989.

Pearce, Joseph. *Small Is Still Beautiful: Economics as if Families Mattered.* Wilmington, DE: ISI Books, 2006.

Ramsey, Dave. *The Total Money Makeover: A Proven Plan for Financial Fitness.* Nashville, TN: Thomas Nelson, 2009.

Rolheiser, Ronald. *The Holy Longing: The Search for a Christian Spirituality.* New York: Doubleday, 1999.

Rule of Saint Benedict 1980. Edited by Timothy Fry. Collegeville, MN: Liturgical Press, 1981.

Russell, A. J., ed. *God Calling.* Uhrichsville, OH: Barbour Publishing, 1989.

Teresa of Avila. *Interior Castle.* Edited and translated by E. Allison Peers. Mineola, NY: Dover Publications, 2007.

———. *The Way of Perfection.* Edited by Henry L. Carrigan Jr. Brewster, MA: Paraclete Press, 2000.

Tolle, Eckhart. *The Power of Now: A Guide to Spiritual Enlightenment.* Novato, CA: New World Library, 2004.

United States Conference of Catholic Bishops. Economic Justice for All. Pastoral Letter on Catholic Social Teaching and the U.S. Economy. Washington, DC: USCCB Publishing, 2009.

———. For I Was Hungry and You Gave Me Food: Catholic Reflections on Food, Farmers, and Farmworkers. Washington, DC: USCCB Publishing, 2003.

———. Stewardship: A Disciple's Response. A Pastoral Letter on Stewardship. Tenth Anniversary Edition. Washington, DC: USCCB Publishing, 2002.